Dear Dad

Dear Dad

Reflections on Fatherhood

John W. Fountain

WESTSIDE PRESS

CHICAGO

For information, address WestSide Press, 27 N. Wacker Drive, Suite 428,
Chicago, IL 60606.

Book cover design by Laura Sebold
Book design and composition by Mark McGarry

Library of Congress Control Number: 2010933458
Fountain, John W., 1960–
Dear Dad: Reflections on Fatherhood /
by John W. Fountain. — 1st ed.
ISBN 9780981485898

For Mama,
who, even in my father's absence,
never abandoned ship.

Contents

About the Book

This project was inspired by my essay for National Public Radio's *This I Believe* series and is itself a compilation of true narratives written by a group of journalists and writers I assembled for this project. Men and women from various walks of life and various generations, they are black, white, and Hispanic. A good number of them have written for some of the nation's best news organizations—the *New York Times, Chicago Tribune, Washington Post, Time* magazine, and others. All of them write in the pages that follow about the impact of fathers, and also fatherlessness, on their own lives. This comes at a time when the focus of a national initiative and even President Barack Obama have sounded the clarion call for responsible fatherhood amid a continuing crisis of paternal absenteeism.

Fatherhood is a subject that deserves our attention. A key component of that critical socializing agent known as family, "father" is important to us all.

So what better time than this—than now—to lend to and perhaps spur the national dialogue on fatherhood, to raise to the light images of the best of our fathers, and also examples of some failed or flawed fathers, with the hope that from each may be gleaned a more perfect model to which all fathers might aspire? And there seems no better way to examine fatherhood and to extract lessons from the past in the hope of creating a brighter future than to follow the reflective journeys of writers who remember their fathers lovingly, poignantly, vividly, at times longingly, even sometimes with disappointment.

Through the prism of our collective lens, these mini-memoirs recall time we spent with our fathers, or in some cases, the lack thereof. And each seeks to provide insights on the best of fathering, if not also hope for the millions of American children who today face growing up in homes with no father present.

What we present here are hardly religious sermons. They are instead stories steeped in journalistic craft, stories that resonate deeply on the universal themes of childhood, family, struggle, love, and loss, offering a kind of collective case study. They are stories that I—that we—believe have the potential by the power of intimate narrative not only to help others understand the impact of fatherlessness but also to help mend those most wounded.

These stories are not black, or white, or brown. They are not singularly male or female, nor are they solely American. Rather, they are transcendent stories about the human condition, about the human spirit and the universal longing to feel connected to who we are, and *whose* we are, to that critical figure we all know as father and to the lasting lessons our fathers taught us, by their presence, or by their absence.

In some ways, this book is also a tribute to fathers, a celebration and remembrance of those men who have graced our lives with paternal love and guidance, whether or not they were our natural fathers. It is a tribute to those special men who had the courage, faith, and fortitude to withstand the storms of their own lives and yet remain resolved to produce, protect, and provide for their families.

This book is for everyone who has a father, for everyone who has lost one, loved one, or longed for one, for everyone who happens to be one, and for everyone who longs to be a better one.

And finally, this book is for everyone who longs to make peace with one—a gift to all good fathers past, present, and future, and sealed with a prayer for them all.

JOHN W. FOUNTAIN

Prologue

In the absence of my father, I have longed at times in my life for affirmation, for the steadying hand on the shoulder; for the paternal love that is reassuring, establishing, uplifting, grounding, life-giving—only to find none. This deficit in my upbringing was devastating.

I am the son of mostly de facto fathering, of the pieces and particles that fell from the cloaks of men who filed past my life, men whose paths crossed with mine or with whom I walked for a time. But I cannot say with certainty whether it was the case that those men closest to me would not or could not promote me, or whether they never fully embraced or fully esteemed me, at those particular times in my life. What I can say and what I do know is that as a result, for much of my life I felt fatherless.

Strangely, perhaps—and at least certainly this was unexpected—I eventually found solace and healing in my reflections as an adult upon the frailties of all fathers, including my own frailties as a man; in the forgiving of those men whom I deem to have in ways failed me; and also in my own journey of fatherhood and my willingness to provide paternal nurturing and substance to my own children and even those who are the seed of other men. I have found strength and a measure of healing in my earnest desire to be a better father and a better man than my own natural father and to learn as I travel this course from the mistakes of others and those I have made myself.

Still, there is a hole, a feeling of emptiness, in a certain place in my heart, a place that was meant to be filled with a lifetime of memories made with my father. I suspect there always will be. And yet I have found strength in the presence of an Eternal Father, and in that good gained from even the imperfect men I encountered from boyhood to manhood. And though I remember not the joy of my own father taking delight in me, now I do know and embrace the joys as well as the responsibility of fatherhood.

And there is a part of me—the little boy in me—who finds in me the kind of father he always wished he had. That has always been my endeavor, my promise to myself as a little boy, a promise I intend to keep until my last breath.

Someone once advised me during one of life's inevitable storms not to "despise the process." In other words, the sometimes painful struggles of life and their accompanying heartaches and sufferings can ultimately create in us a heart that seeks to heal and help others. I have come to believe that as we pass through our sufferings and survive them, the lessons learned through our own healing can ultimately serve a greater purpose: the healing of others, the mending of broken hearts, perhaps even the healing of a nation.

This project incubated during the years of hurt and eventual healing from the paternal desertion I experienced in my own life. It was, in fact, an essay I wrote in 2004 for National Public Radio's *This I Believe* series about the absence of my father and what "saved" me, and ultimately the responses that subsequently poured in from around the country from people of all walks of life that led me to consider writing more on the subject. That piece appears in this collection along with several others I have written over the years, in some cases as narrative, and in others, as poetic essays or letters.

The responses to the NPR essay—moving and deeply contemplative—touched me and reaffirmed the depths of the impact of fatherlessness, but even more, they affirmed the need of many others for healing. One of those responses was from a gentleman on the East Coast who said he had heard the essay and wondered if I might send him a few pictures to accompany the NPR podcast, which he had played for a Christian group of mentor-educators who frequently encountered young men and women growing up without a father. I strung together a series of photographs from my childhood, including the only picture I have of my biological father—a faded portrait frozen in time of a smiling man with his hat half-cocked and the swollen lines of alcoholism beneath his eyes and in his gaunt cheeks. I arranged that photograph and also a few of me, as well as some accompanying video clips, coordinated them with the NPR podcast, and sent it along. I understand that the Christian group continues today to show the clip, which has become a tool for training.

I also show the five-minute video clip, mostly to groups of youths and to church men's ministries. It is part of what the saints at my grandfather's Pentecostal church would call my "testimony." And without fail, after having shown the video, the responses pour from the mouths and eyes of those for whom the words of that essay strike a chord, particularly from males, regardless of age or race: a teary young man in a Baptist church in Kentucky; a man driving in his car along a city street; students in a university classroom; or homeless men and women at a Thanksgiving gathering inside a Chicago shelter.

Not long ago, while speaking at that shelter run by a Christian ministry, I showed the video clip. Soon after the closing prayer had ended, a fortyish, burly man with a round brown face approached me and began to share how much what I had said had touched him. He had, in fact, been moved to tears. He, too, had grown up without knowing his father. Then one day after he became an adult, he finally met him. Sometime later, he and his father got into an argument, he explained as I listened intently. They argued, he said—he and his father. Then it happened.

"He shot me in the mouth," he said matter-of-factly before melting again into tears.

On one side of his mouth, he bore the scar to prove it. But what I understood as we stood there was that his scars and his pain ran much deeper. I also understood that they would be eternally his to carry, were there no hope of healing.

I explained to the brother that day that there is a father who is infallible and loving. That He is a father who, though He be of spirit and invisible, and not of flesh and blood or tangible, is a father no less. That this Father I have found is able to comfort, console, and embrace his sons and daughters with a love and peace far beyond human understanding. He is a father who stands with one foot in the beginning of time and the other in eternity. He is a sovereign Father who allows our earthly fathers to choose to be good fathers, or not. And He is a Father who also finds no shortage of means by which to care for those of us who find ourselves paternally abandoned or disconnected, sinking for what seems like the last time in deep consuming waters that encompass our souls. He is God the Father. God, my Father. God, our Father.

In constructing this volume, I searched my mind and experience for stories of other writers I have met or known through my work as a newspaper journalist for more than twenty years. Mostly, they are people with whom I had shared over the course of our friendship bits and pieces of my childhood experiences. I began to make calls or send e-mails to inquire whether they might be interested in contributing to this project. Before too long, a group of writers emerged.

There is Nichole Christian, formerly on the editorial board of the *Detroit Free Press*, whom I met first when I was a reporter at the *Chicago Tribune* and later worked with when we were both staff writers at the *New York Times*. There is Sylvester Monroe, formerly a *Newsweek* and *Time* magazine correspondent and newspaperman, at one time senior editor at *Ebony* magazine. There is Rosa Maria Santana, a former *Chicago Tribune* colleague and writer for the *Cleveland Plain Dealer*. There is Mario Parker, a correspondent for *Bloomberg News* and the *Washington Post*'s Hamil Harris. There is my good friend Vincent Allen, a career U.S. marine, pastor, and founder of Agape Ministries in Stafford, Virginia. There is my friend and former journalism colleague Lee Bey, formerly a reporter-columnist for the *Chicago Sun-Times*. There are fifteen writers, not including myself, whose stories appear in this volume. I am grateful to all of them for pouring a piece of their souls onto these public pages.

Most important in my selecting of these writers, as has been the case with those people I have chosen to write about for more than two decades as a newspaperman, is that they each have a story to tell. But in this case, it was equally important that the subjects, in the vein of the Black Church's oral tradition of testifying, be able to tell or to write their own stories in their own resonant voices, using the vehicle of narrative writing. Also, rather than to seek to tell the stories of the rich and famous or notable, and in doing so, to risk—at least in my view—the element of "celebrity" taking precedence over the story, I felt led to focus on the stories of somewhat ordinary men and women. In this way, I hoped to provide a common access point for ordinary people to examine the issue of fatherhood and fatherlessness through the fabric of their own unique cultural experiences.

For anyone who has ever known the agony of fatherlessness, there is no need to delineate its effects. Nor is there any quick prescription for healing—no clear-cut cure for the hurts suffered due to the lack of paternal nurturing and love. And for those who have known a father's love and presence, the impact is in many ways immeasurable. In America today, millions of boys and girls, U.S. Census figures show, live in homes absent their biological father. In far too many cases, they live without any semblance of this figure so essential to our emotional, physical, and spiritual well-being. There is no greater issue confronting our children, our communities, and our country. Collectively, the writers in this volume know this well.

Some writers in this volume wrestle with the absence of their fathers while growing up—with paternal desertion, with paternal neglect, abuse, or dysfunction, or with the emotional disengagement of their fathers. Others deal with the loss of their father's mortal presence due to death or incapacitation. And others fondly recall the fathers they dearly love, the making of memories with them, and the learning of lessons that will endure for a lifetime. For among these stories are moving tributes to good and faithful fathers and to all men who choose to be a good and present influence in their children's lives.

There are stories here of good men who chose to be good fathers, not only to their own children but also to their communities. There are stories of reconnection, stories of reconciliation, redemption, and revelation, stories of healing, and of triumph—stories that also speak so clearly to the importance of mothers and grandmothers, who for many of us were our saving grace.

In this volume, there is the story of the father who died months after his drug-addicted ex-wife succumbed to an overdose, leaving behind a child with a million unanswered questions; the truth leads to an unraveling of the hero she had always believed her dad to be, but it also provides the thread to longed-for answers, to peace and resolution about the man she only thought she knew. There is the story of the granddaughter who finds within a bullet hole in a basement wall a window to the past and memories of a loving grandfather. There is the story of the young black boy who loses his father, and his discovery of their eternal connection, of the paternal lessons that can endure for a lifetime, of that bond that indeed transcends even death. There is the absentee father and the impact of his cold disconnection on a little girl who found through his absence the drive and motivation to rise beyond her circumstance to educational and professional heights, and ultimately consolation. There is the story of the little boy who found more consistency in a drill sergeant than in his alcoholic father. There are the stories of invisible fathers, stories of paternal heartache perhaps more than any one soul should have to bear. There is my own story, the story of a father who died drunk and the story of my own search for solace and reconciliation and my discovery of a God who embraced me. And there is the story of the father and son, separated by years, miles, and the unknown through no fault of their own, and the fateful telephone call that led to their reunion, a baseball game, and the chance for them both as men by then to mend their ties.

This is not a "bash fathers" book. Nor are the stories tell-all exposés. But you will find no perfect men.

There are also no victims here in our collective psalm, only victors.

In some ways, this is a how-to manual: How to overcome. How to succeed. How to live on. How to be a better father. How to forgive our fathers.

We write with the understanding that so many boys and girls across America each day face through no fault of their own the void left by fatherlessness. We set down our words with the knowledge that so many men still have the power to heal by charting a new course in fatherhood. We write in hope of reversing that curse often passed down by the absence or complete failure of fathers. We are also fully aware that even as we breathe, we shape the histories of our own children's experience with father—or mother—and ourselves are subject to human frailty. We write to encourage good fathers who feel undervalued and underappreciated to stay the course. We write to celebrate fatherhood.

Our hope is that others may find somewhere in these pages a guidepost—at least a beacon to reflect light on their own paternal pasts.

Perhaps it is too much to hope that others might find in our stories some measure of healing. But one can hope.

For anyone who has ever felt like a fatherless child, that is our hope as we write in the pages that follow, reflecting with deep sentiment on these two simple words: "Dear Dad."

Reflection

Honour thy father...
Exodus 20:12

Anne Valente as a child with her grandfather.

An Open Letter to a Father: Dear Dad

John W. Fountain

Written Father's Day, 1996

Dear Dad,

I'm sitting here at the computer this morning writing this letter. Since college and stuff, it's just a lot easier for me to use the computer rather than write by hand, that's all. Imani and Monica are fine. The Bulls look terrible. I can't believe the Sonics have won two games. Man oh man.

I hope everybody there is fine. I miss you all and pray that one day God will open the door for me to come back home, for good.

Sitting here this morning, I am filled with emotion. On Father's Days in the past I have felt the same kind of things, but really have not been able to come to grips with my feelings. It's just really hard sometimes to do that and even harder to talk about it. But I'm going to try anyway:

I have at times in my life been very angry with you. Not necessarily for how you treated me, but how you treated my mother. I have been so very angry. But not only angry, I have been disappointed, troubled and hurt. I have found that those feelings have at times covered up everything good I felt about you. All the things you have done for me. The times when you were there for me. When you were the only man in my life that I could really turn to for help, for support.

I have been angry about the times when as a child we would wait at home for you to come home from work and we would be hungry. The times when I would as a kid clean up the house because I felt like if I did that, then you wouldn't have anything to fuss about and you and Mama wouldn't fight. I felt like you could have been a better husband, a better man, a better father. And many of my feelings of anger and hurt, I carried with me to adulthood, no matter how hard I tried to push them aside. I cannot lie to you. I cannot say that I still don't feel them sometimes. At 35, it still makes me cry. And I really wish I could wipe all of that ugliness away with all the hurt and pain and anger and erase that part of our past. But I can't. And I believe that if you could go back and change some things, you would. But you can't.

So where does that leave us? I don't know. I do know that despite the anger and hurt, I know that I love you. You are the only Dad I know. When I needed money, you have always been more than willing to give it to me. When I needed you to be somewhere for me or give me a ride or whatever, you were always there.

And you know, since I have gotten older, I have come to understand that it ain't so easy being the man of the house. It's tough. And there have been many times I have wanted to run away. Too much responsibility. Too tough. I imagine that you must have felt like that, too, sometimes. But you stayed. And I respect you for that.

I've also learned that no matter how perfect a father I have tried to be, I have made mistakes. And my sons probably have feelings of hurt and anger about me. Hey, I'm only human. And I realize that so are you. My mistakes didn't mean that I loved my sons or daughters any less. I just made mistakes. I'm still responsible. But I made some mistakes, and I hope my sons will forgive me. And I want you to know that I do forgive you.

This being-a-daddy stuff isn't easy. I have four kids and still can't believe it. I imagined the other day what it must have been like for you as a young man, married with several kids, two of them not your own biological children. I wondered what dreams you had as a young man. What you had hoped to become. And I thought about all the sacrifices you made for us. The times when you were there for us. Through disappointment. Through pain. Through marriage. And those feelings of hurt and anger I talked about earlier seemed to fade away. I thought about how you taught me to drive, how when I messed up the green LeSabre you never said a word about it (I don't think I would have been as patient with my own sons). I thought about some fun times. How you taught me how to use your baseball glove. About your tender nature with children and about whipping your butt in table hockey and checkers (I did win a few games).

It's funny how often in relationships we dwell on the bad. On the pain. I guess it's only human because we are most hurt by the folks who mean the most to us. But in my heart this morning is the joy of knowing a man who was not my natural father, but who was there many, many times that I needed him.

When Monica tells me how handy I am around the house, I tell her that it is because of you. When I am playing with Imani, making faces, laughing, calling her names, I hear a piece of you in me. When I say, "Too late for the camel, 'cause the pig's got his eyes closed" (whatever that means), I hear you. I sometimes hear Santana, Bobbie Gentry, the old southern sound of the Mississippi Delta blues, and I hear you. And I realize that you are a part of me because you are my dad.

I'm still working on being a better man, a better father, a better husband. I hope and pray that you are too. Regardless, I still love you.

Your Son,
John

Dad's Lesson: Life Is About Now, Not Then

Donald A. Hayner

In the morning, I say good-bye to my dad from inside the clean and cheerful confines of the nursing home where he lives. It's an assisted-living home for Alzheimer's patients. Mornings are always best. His thoughts are clearest. We'll sit together, or walk through the gardens outside. I often find myself studying his face. Some days, he looks old and remotely recognizable. Other days, he looks like the dad I remember as a kid, the same guy I saw walking across my high school athletic field thirty-three years ago.

"I was a sprinter on the track team, practicing starts, when I heard a teammate say, "Who's this? Some Olympic scout coming to check me out?"

I looked up and saw my dad. *Why wasn't he at work,* I wondered. He was wearing a business suit and trench coat. He was short, built like a bulldog, with a marine's crew cut and an all-business walk. He gently motioned me to join him.

He didn't say why until we were inside the family car. Then, he told me my brother was dead. He had committed suicide in his college dorm room. As he drove me home, I looked out the window, away from him, and cried. It was a short ride. I think it was raining.

Walking inside our house seemed a lot different now. My mother was devastated, crying in my brother's room, lost and bewildered. Friends and family came by, all offering various explanations of my brother's death. I mostly just stayed in my room.

At one point, I remember my dad sitting in a living room chair. Here was a man who was always fearless, a tough guy who worked in the steel mills for thirty years. As he sat talking, his chest suddenly started to heave with waves of grief from deep inside.

That was the first time I saw him cry.

My father had his share of hurt in life. When he was twelve, he and his brother were rescued from a second-story window as the family house burned down, killing his father. His brother died in Casablanca in World War II. And now he had lost a son.

My brother was buried on my sixteenth birthday, and I went back to school and back to living my life, sort of. It was just the three of us now. I was now an only child, and we were a different family. Grief hung on us like wet clothes.

We all seemed to be living in a kind of slow motion, rehashing my brother's life over and over, trying to find some answer. I was angry for what my brother had done—and filled with grief, guilt, and regret. This went on for weeks, the three of us living in a fog.

Then, one day, as we were sitting in the kitchen talking, my father gave me some advice, the kind of advice you should hear on Father's Day.

"As you know, I loved your brother completely and always will," he said, "but now it's time. It's time to move on, to live again. There is no alternative. I'm going to move on, and I suggest you join me."

That was it. It didn't make the sorrow go away. But it stirred the right stuff inside and was said by the right man at the right time.

Life is about now and not then. Full speed ahead, no matter what. That, ultimately, is my dad's legacy to me. I think about that every time I see him and talk with him. He never complained, he always talked about how well he was doing, or the beauty of where he was living or how much he was loved.

Acknowledge the defeats, but push on. And always, always celebrate the victories.

My dad has buried two wives he loved and now is lost in the confusion of sometimes forgetting who he is. But the spark is there, even through the mist. When my dad recently entered the assisted-care home, I had to fill out a questionnaire that asked about his personality.

"Dad," I said, "they asked me to describe you as an optimist or pessimist. What do you think I said?"

"Optimist," he said, answering immediately.

"That's right," I said. "That's right."

Don Hayner's dad passed away in 2002.

DONALD A. HAYNER—Editor in chief of the *Chicago Sun-Times*, Hayner has been a general assignment reporter, a personal finance writer, a neighborhood beat reporter, and a Sunday features writer. He became the city editor, metro editor, and then managing editor. He has also coauthored three books. Hayner is a graduate of Ripon College and John Marshall Law School. After three years of practicing law, Hayner switched careers and went to work as a reporter at City News Bureau. From there he went to the *Suburban Tribune*, where he was a reporter and later a columnist. He is married, has two sons, and lives on Chicago's South Side.

The Truth at Last

Nichole Christian

Years after my daddy died, I finally laid down my superhero image of him, too. Two decades after spreading his ashes, facts I'd never known about Daddy began to surface and collide with the fiction I had cherished as a child. It turns out Daddy was more human than I could ever see.

It's funny to me now the way I once romanticized a man I knew so little about. And sometimes I cringe, thinking of the many nights, the many ways I prayed death upon my mother, while forgetting and forgiving Daddy, who'd gone AWOL first.

He had ducked out of their marriage not long after doing the honorable thing and marrying my pregnant mother. By the time I was fourteen, they were both dead, departing one after the other—first her (by a drug overdose), then him, with just nine months between them.

Through it all, Daddy remained golden to me because he was the one who bothered to come around. My mother had parked me at her parents' house while she divided her time between getting high and her stints in jail for petty robberies. I never understood how he knew, but Daddy always managed to show up when she was at her worst. The more he showed up, the more people swore they saw him in me: his eyes, his chin, his highbrow humor. Daddy bought me Underoos—*Bat-girl* and *Wonder Woman*—before anyone on the block had a pair.

I saw *E.T.* on the big screen, with Daddy at my side. He plied me with buttered popcorn, while I pretended not to see his little brown paper bag or to smell the stench seeping from it every time he raced it up to his lips. One parent playing the part here and there was better than none at all. Even now, I smile at the memory of Daddy bopping up the street, sing-calling the nickname he created just for me. "Cola, Cola," Daddy would sing.

In my childhood eyes, the precious moments he'd given me seemed the measure of a man worth worshiping. I was content with the things I knew about my father. That is, until many years later when I myself became a parent and started sifting through the details I'd one day tell my daughter. I wanted to be able to share with her the good stuff, a way to understand why I was so proud to be Daddy's girl. I wanted to pour the details into a letter for her to read someday as I'd done with so many of the tales about my family and our struggles.

The year she turned three, I called Uncle Raymond—Daddy's brother—looking to flesh out a story I'd heard bits and pieces of that had always made me proud. Daddy had been a soldier in Korea, so the story went. I had seen a grainy old photo of him once in what looked like a soldier's uniform. I had imagined him a decorated soldier in the war who had been too torn up to tell his story. Uncle Raymond, I had decided, would give me the facts.

"Daddy was in the war, how long?" I asked Uncle Raymond over the telephone.

Uncle Raymond's voice went silent. I could hear him take a quick breath. It should have been my clue that I had just stuck the key into Pandora's box.

"Your daddy *was* in the army, got in 1956," he said, his voice placing special emphasis on the word "was." He continued:

"But he did more time in the army jail than he did in service, 'bout two years. He got caught smuggling weed. He was 'sleep on a truck crossing a border somewhere with smoke in his pocket. The fellas with him forgot to wake him up. That's how they got him."

Uncle Raymond's words got me. He could sense as much. "You don't believe me, do you?" he said.

"What else don't I know?" I asked respectfully.

"Well," he said, "your daddy used to be a pimp. He'd have his girls out there doing their thing. He was making the money, went from hustling weed to cutting and selling heroin. It was normal in our day to want to be a numbers man, a player, a pimp. And he was good at it, making $2,000 a week."

My uncle's tales knocked me back in my chair. The picture he was painting didn't fit the man I remembered. The man I loved. The man I knew in my heart, though I could sense instantly that my uncle's tales were true.

There was also that one shred of corroboration I had seen my entire life: Daddy's hands. They'd always told his business. They were swollen and dented, scarred by years of shooting dope. This I knew, even as a child. But I chose to believe Daddy had made a mistake and had spent the rest of his life struggling to do better, floating in and out of construction jobs and feting me with gifts whenever his money allowed. Never once did I suspect the hold that drugs apparently had on his life.

Still, I had no reason to doubt Uncle Raymond. Even before Daddy died, my uncle had stepped in as surrogate. He lived around the corner from my grandparents. I would go to his house when I wanted to get a message to Daddy. During the summer, I made a beeline for his front porch, where he was always aching to teach me something. He taught me to play backgammon and chess, opened my eyes to the power of positive thinking with his nutty New Age mantras, and gave me my first paying job as his sidekick when he launched a business selling hot tamales at the post office. The business failed. But I soared under the attention. Our bond was real, and I doubted Uncle Raymond would jeopardize it by badmouthing his little brother.

Still, I couldn't easily swallow all that he had told me. Every time I tried, I tripped over a larger question that shook me to my core. And there was for me one question that begged for an answer more than any other, one that made me tremble, even as I asked it:

"Did my daddy get my mother hooked?"

Uncle Raymond's answer came quick.

"I'm not sure," he said. "But," he added, "there is someone you should meet who might know."

Then Uncle Raymond made me promise to attend his Labor Day barbecue to meet a mystery man named "Frank" (not his real name), whom he swore would know all of Daddy's secrets. He was his oldest living friend and had been his partner in crime. I told Uncle Raymond I'd be there, even if privately I dreaded learning more.

Though my Daddy died believing I loved him best, after Uncle Raymond's revelations my own pride in being his daughter had been wounded. In an instant, I had become a recovering daddy's girl. I didn't hate him. But I could no longer hold him up as my parental saving grace, not when I knew there was still more to the story.

On the day Frank and I were to meet in a treeless backyard under a scorching sun, I decided to treat the meeting like an assignment. I pretended to leave my emotions at home and arrived instead with the tools of my trade: pen, paper, and a long list of questions. Moving through the crowd, I was determined to spot him first. I did. I could tell by his hands. They were a mirror image of Daddy's, pitted and pockmarked.

We shook. He spoke first.

"She looks like him," Frank said more to Uncle Raymond than to me. Frank was tall, slim, and slow talking, careful with his words and trying just as carefully to cover up his missing teeth.

"Ray says, you want to know 'bout your daddy's younger days," he said.

I nodded. He launched right in, filling in the details I had never known.

"He always wanted to get himself together, but you got to understand, we started getting high at twelve years old ..."

The lump in my throat wouldn't allow me to look Frank in the eye. I focused instead on my pen, tracking it back and forth across the page.

"We took a lot of stupid chances, but we didn't hurt nobody, the way guys do today. We started out just helping the older guys move their stuff. And the money got good for us, too. We had the best of everything: cashmere coats, hats, and girls. Sometimes on a good week, we'd take everybody to the show—ten, twelve people. Bernard was big-hearted like that."

Frank's eyes were locked on me. I tried to stare back without judging, without crying.

There was that nagging question.

"Did you know my mother, Barbara?" I asked.

"Yeah, she was something else—tough," he said. "But she wasn't the love of his life. They got together 'cause he got her pregnant."

His words hit hard. Still, I pressed for more.

"Did he start her using, too?" I asked.

This time neither of us looked away.

"Wish I could say no. But things was wild back then," he said matter-of-factly. "Who knows?"

I had hoped Frank could tell me for certain. But in a way, his empty answer gave me something richer—a reason and the moment to accept my mother and my daddy for what and who they were: two flawed human beings, not a hero among them, simply the two people who gave me life.

I'm glad I finally see.

NICHOLE CHRISTIAN—A native Detroiter, she was formerly a member of the *Detroit Free Press* editorial board, writing about education policy and children's issues. She began her career at the *St. Petersburg Times* and later became a staff writer at the *Wall Street Journal*, the *New York Times*, and *Time* magazine, where she was Detroit bureau chief. As a reporter at the *New York Times*, Christian was among the reporters on the newspaper's metro staff who produced "Portraits of Grief," chronicling the lives of people killed in the September 11 attacks. Christian wrote fifty of those portraits, part of the *Times's A Nation Challenged* special section, which was awarded the 2002 Pulitzer Prize for public service.

Cutting My Son's Hair:
A Priceless, Intimate Moment

John W. Fountain

The cost was just $5.00. So I grabbed two. Two sets of electric shears for my father-and-son ritual, though I now only have one little boy's hair to cut. My own hair has succumbed to cowlicks and age, and is easily cleared with a straight-edge razor and shaving cream in the shower.

"Hey, I can't believe this price. I think I'll get two," I said to my mother, speaking on my BlackBerry. "I can cut Malik's hair until he's nineteen."

My son Malik is seven. I gave him his first haircut as he sat in a high chair in our kitchen, cupping his head in my hands while he wept and his big sister pestered him, not long after he had taken his first steps. Malik is my third and youngest son. The others are grown now—going on thirty-one and twenty-nine. When they were small, I cut their hair, too. My stepfather cut mine as a boy.

Cutting my boys' hair was first a matter of necessity, though it became a ritual between father and sons, one that still holds deep meaning for me, a collection of priceless intimate moments that will last a lifetime. And in a time when I see so many fathers neglecting the time, missing irredeemable, precious moments with their children, I cannot help but shake my head.

I became a father at seventeen. Short on funds, and understanding the necessity to keep my boys well groomed—just as important for their self-esteem as it was to my sense of duty as a father—I decided that I should buy a set of clippers and teach myself to cut hair. I must have paid about $30.00 or so for that first set. I could barely afford it but figured that after only a couple of cuts, it would pay for itself.

The cost paid by my boys was a different matter. They mostly suffered silently through my learning pains: edgings so far back on their heads they appeared cowlick-stricken, painful nicks and plugs made by sudden slips of my hand, or craters in their short Afros that sometimes rose like peaks and valleys as I struggled to cut their hair evenly. Then there were the high-top fades, some of which on my eldest son, until I had perfected them, looked like Gumby makeovers.

And yet each time I called for them to meet me in a room for our ritual, they came. Truth is, they didn't have a choice, though sometimes I suspected they would much rather have sat in a real barber's chair. The year my boys and I lived in a quaint English countryside town with my new wife, who was a British Marshall scholar, my barber skills—still being perfected—came in handy. It also saved us a ton as I buzzed their heads in the living room, Lewes Castle glowing just beyond our window.

Later, even when I did have the money and my available time was severely taxed by work and other responsibilities, I still opted to cut my boys' hair, drawn by then by the intimacy of the ritual—the solo time with my sons, talking face-to-face, cradling their heads, meticulously and carefully grooming them from boyhood to adolescence to nearly adulthood, knowing that time and life and space would eventually stand between us.

It was not always easy to find the time to cut their hair. I found instead that I had to *take* the time.

That has been the most fundamental task of fatherhood, even when I have been low on funds: To take the time—to cut hair, to throw a ball, to visit a classroom, to talk or just to sit together in silence. To understand that while material substance is important, nothing outweighs a man's ability and willingness to touch his sons—and daughters—tenderly, gently, innocently as a father, by his presence in their lives, to look into their eyes and say, "I love you." To show by his actions, even more than by his words, "I love you."

And yet I see so many boys—and girls—nowadays, for whom father has become the invisible man. And I see fathers whose disappearing acts leave their children longing for his touch—men who have allowed their disconnection from their children's mothers, for whatever reason, to divide them from their own flesh and blood.

Upon my divorce from my oldest sons' mother eighteen years ago, I understood that divorce had nothing to do with fatherhood. So that even when maintaining my relationship with my children was made rocky by the static that often occurs between estranged parents, this much I understood: I could not abandon ship—as my father had, so long ago that I have trouble remembering his face.

I do remember walking hand in hand with him once as a little boy, and the sense of security, safety, and solace that filled me. And though I am forty-eight now and my father is thirty years sleeping in his grave, I still long for his breath, just to feel his touch.

My children, I have vowed, won't know that pain.

I cup Malik's head in my hands, then brush his hair neatly into a sheen as I complete a fresh cut and my hands smooth lilac aftershave over his hairline and neck. This is our bond.

One more haircut down. And, I hope, years of many more to go.

Through a Picture Window

Stephanie Gadlin

"I'm gone!" Daddy's words hung in the air like stale cigar smoke. I was about seven years old when my father spat them toward my mother and pulled the door shut forever on our small family. Days would turn into months before I would see my daddy again. No one ever uttered the word "divorce" in our house, but I knew from eavesdropping on my mother's telephone conversations that something in their marriage had gone horribly wrong. One of them no longer loved the other, and so, one of them just had to go. Daddy was not some Shakespearean actor, rehearsing the scene from someone else's life. He was indeed gone— perhaps forever from the woman he once had loved, from all of us, from me. But for a while, I was hopeful. I knew he would return one day. This would not be how our movie ended. And until that time, my kid brother and I resolved to sit in the living room picture window, watching the cars roar down Loomis Boulevard, hoping one of them would bring our daddy back to us.

In time, and with Dad not yet having pulled up in front of our house in his brand-new Buick Skylark to collect us, I told my kid brother that Daddy had been delayed by some great adventure. Surely, he was scaling Mount Kilimanjaro or fighting mummies at the base of the great pyramids. When I got really creative, I spun an intricate tale of great mystery and intrigue, telling my brother that Daddy was really a secret agent man, having been commissioned by President Jimmy Carter to use espionage, Jedi mind tricks, and Bruce Lee's kung fu to help save the world from invading Martians.

Though I tried to convince my brother, truth is, neither of us believed my tales any more than we believed that once a year some fat white man in a red suit broke into our house and left Christmas presents by the couch. The plain truth of the matter was that Daddy had divorced "us." And now, he was gone.

In my bed, I cried. And I sometimes wondered if my father had found another daughter and if he loved her more than he loved me. When I could find no answers, I grew angry, sullen, and deeply introspective, sometimes turning my childish wrath upon my mother. All I knew was that Mama and Daddy now composed two enemy camps, though I could not exactly tell which of them was the friend and which the enemy. No one told me whose side God was on. No one kept the peace. My brother and I were the casualties of my parents' war.

Much later, I read that divorcing families have included more than 1 million children every year from 1972 to 1990, according to the National Center for Health Statistics. My brother and I were two of them, having joined the ranks of officially divorced kids around 1974. Psychologists say it is not divorce in itself that most harms children, but rather the tension between divorcing parents, some of whom repeatedly appear before judges to battle over drop-off times or visitation rights.

For nearly ten years, Daddy popped in and out of our lives like a jack-in-the-box. It sometimes felt like being on the losing end of a dice game—sometimes the die came up in your favor, sometimes you just crapped out. I didn't care—I would wind a million boxes or shoot a billion dice just to see my father face to face, to know he cared and had not forgotten his promises to me when I used to sit on his lap and listen to the tall tales of his childhood. But we had no phone number for Daddy. No address. If the house were to catch fire, we wouldn't know how to reach him, at all. What if something happened to Mama? What if something happened to me? Would he know? Would he come?

Daddy's sporadic weekend visits always involved the same routine: load us into the car; complain about how we looked; drive to a nearby relative's house where all of us would sit awkwardly on a couch, looking at one another in near silence; load back into the car; dodge his questions about what Mama was doing now and with whom; drive to the local Burger King (where we could order whatever we wanted); drive us back home; hand us a check, noting "child support payment" in the bottom left corner; and he was gone again. We would wait weeks on end just to start the process all over again.

Once, my brother and I had not seen or heard from Dad in nearly three or four months. Then suddenly one day, after retrieving the mail, we noticed a six-by-nine-inch glossy postcard addressed to us. My fingers gripped its smallness. I recognized my father's perfect penmanship. The postcard was from Dad. He wanted us to know that he was doing fine and that he was on vacation in Orlando, Florida, that he loved us, and that he'd talk to us soon. Signed "Dad." Then I flipped the card over and looked at the picture of juicy Florida oranges, wet and still on the vine. I flipped it back over again and reread my father's cursive writing. And I just stood there, card in hand, staring way past the words, into that empty place his departure had left in my heart. Suddenly, rage soared through my spirit. It was an emotion I had never experienced before and not until many years later as an adult would I fully understand whence it came.

I balled up that postcard with all of my might and hurled it to the floor. And after I deemed that it still had not been sufficiently destroyed, I picked it up again and tore it into little pieces. Here we were wondering, hoping, praying about him, and there he was, gallivanting with Mickey Mouse. My brother and I had never been to Orlando, the home of Disney World. And wasn't that a place where parents—daddies— took their kids—their little girls? *Whose kids had he taken, if not us?* I wondered.

Was one of them a skinny girl with glasses who devoured books by day and wrote her own stories well into the night? Was she holding onto his neck as he lifted her up to get a better look at something just beyond her gaze? Was she eating chocolate ice cream and being scolded for dropping it on her pastel-colored dress? Was she being told every-thing was going to be all right after tumbling and falling and scarring her knee? Was some other little girl now making my daddy laugh with her silly questions, goofy jokes, and funny faces? Was she the one get-ting the piano lessons now? Was he now buying her new storybooks? Was she the one he now took to see Grandma and Granddaddy in Mis-sissippi? Who was this chick? And who did Daddy think he was, treat-ing me and my brother *like stepchildren*? I knew if I ever found *that girl* I would beat her down, strangle her with my own childish grip, and I'd make her suffer, all because she'd stolen my Daddy from me.

Until this day, whenever I think of that postcard from my father, tears spring from my eyes. I wipe them quickly, leaving no trace of them upon my cheek, though feeling the spiritual impact of each drop. And also to this day, I rarely ever buy postcards.

By the time I was a full-blown teenager, I initiated contact with Dad if I needed money for school projects or wanted new clothes. As I neared age eighteen, I was granted access to his phone number. I had also exchanged my loving moniker for the generic "Dad." And though I sought him for finance or killed the time during our short and mun-dane calls by chattering about relatives I barely knew, I never mustered the nerve to speak to him about real father-daughter things. I only called if I had to or with the prodding of my all-forgiving mother.

"Call your father," she'd say from time to time. "You know he loves y'all."

"Yeah, Ma, I know," I'd lie. I did not know that, or at least I didn't be-lieve it.

"Call him right now!"

"I did," I'd fib again. "He ain't home."

I had to lie. I could not tell my mother that the familiar loneliness of missing Dad had been replaced by a strange bitterness. She would never accept that. She wanted us to "honor thy mother and thy father," and that was all there was to it.

No, Dad had left me, his little girl, standing in that living room, con-fused and crying, a long time ago. What was there to talk about?

My brother rarely spoke of our father at all, and he had even less to say to him in his presence when he took us on our Daddy dates. This was not a joint conspiracy between us. Our silent acquiescence to the social distancing our father had himself imposed upon us was all we had to battle the gulf of loss we felt when he left us out of his new life. In a way, I guess, we wanted to somehow hurt him as much as he had hurt us, which shaped us—me—in ways I could never have expected. In many ways the impact has weighed even heavier upon my brother.

As I became a woman and the world showed me the difference between mountaintops and valleys, I taught myself how to hide in plain sight, how to smile, though hurting, how to pretend that all was well when everything around me was falling apart. I trained myself to stay out of the picture window, to limit my dreams in hope of limiting the possibility of pain. It made me overcompensate and settle for much less, for fear of being left behind once again or left alone. Losing my dad made me like that. But what I realize now is that it was neither my father's nor my mother's intent to tear my heart in two places and that things happen, some of them good, some bad. What I realize now is that what happened to my brother and me in the midst of my parents' breakup wasn't really the issue; it was less about us and really more about them dealing—or not dealing with—the brokenness of their own hearts.

My father is not a bad man. In his youth, he was strong and handsome, smart and resourceful. Nobody could use a hammer and nail like him. He came from good stock and is of good character. No matter how big or small his financial contributions were to our upbringing, at least he gave. He did not curse or beat us. Whenever he was around, I felt protected by and connected to the entangled roots of my family tree. In my imagination he was just like Sidney Poitier, the noble do-gooder in the movies who'd never let you down. My father's Buick was his great white horse upon which he could ride onto our block where he would save the day. But in reality, too often he was more like Claude Rains in *The Invisible Man*, lurking just outside the panes of my window—now you see him, now you don't—haunting me, forcing me to fill in all the missing pieces of him. Dad was always just beyond my grasp. And no matter how far I reached, I could not pull him to me.

Someone once asked if I grew up without my father. I cannot truly say. To me, my father was like the sun on prolonged cloudy days—you know it's out there, somewhere, perhaps just beyond your sight. So you don't really worry because you know someday you will see it again. That was Daddy, Dad, my father, the first man I ever loved. He was out there in the world somewhere, thinking of me, fighting to get back to me, loving me, his girl child.

At least this is the story my heart remembers.

STEPHANIE GADLIN—A writer, artist, and social justice activist, she has also worked as international press secretary to the Reverend Jesse L. Jackson, Sr. Gadlin has served as press adviser to a number of national human and civil rights leaders, including Congressman Bobby L. Rush (D–Ill.); she is currently his press secretary and communications director. Her writings have been published by Third World Press and a number of university publishing houses. Gadlin has also worked as magazine editor, beat reporter, and special contributor to BlackPressUSA. She is a playwright and founder of the Nommo Gathering Black Writers Collective in Chicago.

I Know, I Hope, I Wish

Mario D. Parker

The sun beamed brightly on a warm summer day as Jonathan, LeVar, and I played and discussed the things fourth-graders did—new Nintendo games, new toys, new Air Jordans. LeVar said he planned to ask his father to buy him the new Jordans, Jonathan said he would as well. So, naturally, I declared that I would ask the man of my house to do the same.

"He ain't your real daddy!" Jonathan shouted, referring to my stepfather.

I stared off into space, catatonic almost, feeling naked. My tongue was paralyzed.

"Him and your mother *just* got married," Jonathan said, standing next to the peeling stucco on my grandmother's house on Seventeenth Avenue in Maywood, Illinois.

His words felt like bullets whizzing by.

Then LeVar piped in. "Where's your daddy?" he asked gently, almost sympathetically.

"Oh, man, he died when I was real little," I said looking toward a rusty manhole cover in the backyard, where the grass meets the concrete.

My friends and I went on to talk about something else, to play other games in my grandmother's backyard. But the truth was I didn't know who my father was. The truth was I didn't know his name. Truth was, I had never even seen him.

Perhaps my real father was Anthony, my sisters' father—a husky honey-colored man with dark smoker's lips. When I was younger he had been around regularly. Anthony and my mother, my sister and I would take the Chicago Transit Authority's Blue Line to get across and through the city.

Or maybe he was Sammy, a slender, athletically built chocolate-colored man—another man my mother had once dated.

For years, the residue of LeVar's question rang in my eardrums and psyche: *Where's your daddy?*

I wanted the answer for myself, though for much of my childhood it remained elusive.

My mother was sixteen when she had me. My grandmother raised us both. My mother called my grandmother "Mama," so I grew up calling my grandmother the same. My grandmother naturally called my mother by her first name, so I also called her Kim.

To outsiders, I realized this could be confusing. And I wince at the take on this by comedian Chris Rock, who explains during one comedy routine that it's easy to tell if a kid is going to be [messed] up: "If the kid calls his grandmamma 'Mommy' and his mama 'Pam,' he's going to jail," Rock says.

When my mother got married, she and my stepfather lived in the basement of my grandparents' house where we grew up until they found a place of their own. But I stayed behind with my grandmother, only intermittingly spending time with Kim and her husband and left with lingering questions about the identity of the man who was my father.

The subject of my father was taboo. No one in the family spoke about him. Conversations that had the potential of heading down that road were suddenly halted. Once, my mother was flirting with the idea of having my last name changed to my stepfather's. I purposely mentioned this to my grandmother and she went into a conniption.

"He ain't your father!" she said, shaking her head. "You got my last name and that's how it's gonna be." The conversation died there.

My grandmother was tough, not one to be questioned. I recall elementary school when rumors circulated of a kidnapper calling himself "Homey the Clown" after the character on the popular television show *In Living Color.* On one particular day when my grandmother picked up my friends and me, we were talking about the kidnapper.

"I wish some Homey the Clown *would* try to touch one of y'all," she said, her Southern accent reaching a crescendo. "I got a .38 with his name on it," Mama said, raising her purse toward the roof of the car with one hand, clutching the steering wheel of her silver Chevy Monte Carlo with the left.

In the absence of a father, she raised me to be tough as well and to never feel sorry for myself. Still, I received kisses for expected A's on my report card, and I was forced to go to church, no matter how brightly the sun shined or what my friends were doing that day. But my grandmother's love couldn't plug the void that my father left by being absent from the bleachers of my Saturday morning basketball games. After the games, my teammates' fathers would wrap their arms around them and walk out of the gym, stopping to ask the coach what skills they needed to work on together.

"Where's Your Daddy?"

During elementary school, I looked a lot like my mother: the slender face, dark chocolate complexion, pitch-black eyebrows, the need for corrected vision. In high school my features began to morph, and I had more questions about my own identity. It was around that time that my grandmother urged my mother to tell me who my father was.

One day—I don't remember exactly when—she did as we sat in her bedroom. His name is Lester, my mother told me. They had met at my grandfather's church on the South Side of Chicago, she said, then handed me a grainy old Polaroid of them together. All I could decipher were Afros and smiles.

She told me that the man in the photo was my father and that he moved to Seattle shortly after she became pregnant. That was it. She didn't know anything more. And I didn't press her. For even as we sat on the edge of her bed, I could see the toll of the conversation weighing on her as her eyes bounced behind her glasses.

My grandmother told my grandfather of my curiosity, and he subsequently relayed a message to my father's sister, who still attended Union Tabernacle Baptist Church. One afternoon, she called me and I sat on our sun porch, practically pressing the cordless telephone through my ear as Aunt Peggy told me about my father, about the family's history. She would later connect my father and me on a three-way telephone call, allowing me to speak to him for the first time in my life. She would die a few months later. And it was at Aunt Peggy's funeral that I would finally meet my father.

On an uncharacteristically warm Chicago February day in 1996, at the church where he and my mother dated almost exactly sixteen years earlier, I met Lester for the first time.

I sauntered into the church, my heart pounding to a mélange of questions. *Would he accept me? Would I look like him? Do I hug him? Do I punch him?* A stew of emotions swirled inside. Hurt. Anger. Pride. Love. Remorse. Shame. Inadequacy.

My seventy-five-year-old grandfather and I ambled toward the family, past the rows of wooden pews, down the wine-colored carpet, toward the giant cross at the front of the sanctuary as the sun flickered through stained-glass windows. Tall enough to lick salt off my grandfather's head, I wanted to reach out and hold his hand. And in a moment still frozen in my mind, he pointed out my father to me, the way someone does when trying to play matchmaker. We shook hands. Then he yanked me close and hugged me. I sat down next to him, scrunched in between relatives who looked a lot like me, but whose names I didn't know.

Every so often, I would sneak a peek at him to examine his features to try and connect the dots with my own. There were the large hands, the long digits stretching away from the palm like limbs on a tree. There was the elongated forehead, the broad shoulders. Each time that I would glance over, I was met with eyes that looked identical to mine, large dark pupils that can seem to burn through you.

Lester said he would try to establish a relationship and I desperately wanted to believe him. I did believe him.

And so I tried in the days, weeks, and months that followed our first meeting, even as I fought hard to hush the questions to which I had long awaited answers and that pulsed inside my head whenever we would talk on the phone. My intention was to wait to ask them until we reached a comfort level so as not to scare him away.

In the beginning, we talked relatively frequently, every few months or so. Then it was once every other year, if that.

I was a junior in high school when I finally accepted the reality that in the words of rapper Tupac Shakur: "I was looking for a father—he was gone."

And in some ways, I began to embrace the swarm of statistics hovering around me. Statistics that said I was more likely to go to jail, that my grades wouldn't be comparable to those of my peers whose fathers were present, that I was more likely to abuse drugs, to end up a statistic.

Statistics served a dual purpose for me. On the one hand, I embraced them and used them to fuel my fire in school, in life. On the other, I used them in the same way someone with a family history of heart disease or diabetes uses so-called predictors—you have to run harder, be more active, take better care of yourself in order to survive. Even now, as a fully grown man, I still feed the charcoal of stories of successful black men who grew up without fathers into my kiln.

Along the way, I found strength in the bittersweet life songs of other brothers. Back then, just before my high school basketball games, I sometimes bobbed my head to Shaquille O'Neal's "Biological Didn't Bother," in which he raps about his father abandoning him. And someone might have thought I was having a seizure when I first heard rapper Jay-Z rhyme on "Still Got Love for You."

And I still remember watching a *Fresh Prince of Bel-Air* episode— "Papa's Got a Brand New Excuse"—in which Will Smith meets his father, played by Ben Vereen, who abandoned him fourteen years earlier. In that episode, Smith and his father after years finally reconnect. They make plans to spend the summer together. But at the last second, his father shelves the idea.

Smith launches into a tirade to his uncle, in which he lists all of the things he experienced absent his father, from becoming a good basketball player to going on his first date. Then he emotionally declares that he'll graduate from college, become successful, and raise and love a family. He ends his rant by collapsing into his uncle's arms and asking, "How come he don't want me, man?"

Salty tears streamed down my face as I sat watching the television at our kitchen table, longing for the invisible man.

Even today, I see his reflection when I look in the mirror–the light-bulb-shaped head that begins with a slender chin and balloons outward toward my scalp, the hairline that is gradually moon-walking further away from my eyebrows. All are features, I am told, that are staples on my father's side of the family. They are characteristics that I once used to hate because I inherited them from him. And as I grow older, I look more and more like him—a chocolate clone. I accept it. There's nothing I can do about that, but I can, as Will Smith said to his uncle, better myself and do the opposite of what he did.

And yet, every once in a while, I can still hear my friend LeVar's question: *Where's your daddy?*

I hear it when I drift off and daydream about having children some day, or when I imagine them asking about their grandfather, or when my byline pops up in the newspaper, wondering by chance if my father will pick it up and read that particular story, or sometimes simply for no reason at all.

MARIO D. PARKER—A Chicago-based journalist for *Bloomberg News,* he previously reported from the company's Washington, D.C., bureau, before moving to Chicago in 2007. His byline has appeared in newspapers across the globe, including the *Christian Science Monitor, Washington Post, Chicago Tribune, Chicago Sun-Times, International Herald Tribune,* and *New York Times.* In 2008, Parker was a recipient of the Chicago Headline Club's Peter Lisagor Award for Exemplary Journalism. At *Bloomberg,* he covers the developing energy industry, including U.S. energy policy and also general assignment stories across the Midwest. He is a native of Maywood, Illinois.

Ode to a Southern Father:
For Daddy Luther

John W. Fountain

Written as a tribute to my stepfather's father and read in memory at his funeral service, it is a reflection of the best in manhood and a song for many black patriarchs whose lives and very existence go largely unnoticed by the world, though not by those who love them.

If I close my eyes tight
I can still remember
That little house
On a country road.
And all the folks inside
Mama Ada,
Daddy Luther,
And all the Family Pride…
In that little house on the side
Of the road
Back when the Jackson Five still had 'fro's
That summer we chewed tobacco as we strolled down the road
And Jimmy T, Herman Earl and ME
Fished with wooden poles
Before we grew old

Before it was cold
Before it was cold …

Summer fun
Baking-hot asphalt Sun
On barren toes
Cock crowing
Pigs slopping
Green fields where everything grows.
Candy girl's in the kitchen
Helping with the meal
Ollie's already laughin' 'bout somethin'
Everything is re-e-eal
Slo-o-ow
Moving in slow motion,
As I remember the feel
It was real
It was real …

Back then,
By the break of day,
Daddy Luther's already been fishing
Got fish for days
We got fish for days
Chillin' on the ice in the coolers out back
Buffalo, perch and even Cat
And everybody's fine
I remember the time
I remember the time …
In that little house on the side of the road
Back when the Jackson Five still had 'fro's
That summer we chewed tobacco as we strolled down the road
And Jimmy T, Herman Earl and ME
Fished with wooden poles
Before we grew old

Before it was cold
Before it was cold ...

I remember when
That wild dog from down the road
Wouldn't leave those piglets alone
Daddy Luther had left the house
Dog must've thought he was gone.
But under a star-lit sky
That old dog caught his eye
Daddy Luther rushed back
Said, "That dog gon' die."
Then with his loaded shotgun raised just high
Thunder cracked the sky
And that dog did die
That ain't no lie
That ain't no lie ...

It was at that little house on the side of the road
Back when the Jackson Five still had 'fro's
That summer we chewed tobacco as we strolled down the road
And Jimmy T, Herman Earl and ME
Fished with wooden poles
Before we grew old
Before it was cold
Now it's so cold
But I still remember ...
Daddy Luther
So brown, so proud
With a voice like thunder that could crack so loud
Not a whisker out of place whenever he stepped out
I know y'all remember what I'm talking about
Shoes shining
Face smiling
Walk styling

Steps gliding
Him and Mama Ada—embracing—allowing
Never disavowing
A little boy named Fountain
To come into
That little house on the side
Of the road
Back when the Jackson Five still had 'fro's
That summer we chewed tobacco as we strolled down the road
And Jimmy T, Herman Earl and ME
Fished with wooden poles
Before we grew old
Before it was cold
Now it's so cold.
But I still remember.
And Daddy Luther, we love you.

Reconciliation

*And he shall turn the heart of the fathers to the children,
and the heart of the children to their fathers...*
Malachi 4:6

John W. Fountain and his sister Gloria as children.

The God Who Embraced Me

John W. Fountain

I believe in God. Not that cosmic, intangible spirit-in-the-sky that Mama told me as a little boy "always was and always will be." But the God who embraced me when Daddy disappeared from our lives—from my life at age four, the night police leading him away from our front door, down the stairs in handcuffs.

The God who warmed me when we could see our breath inside our freezing apartment, where the gas was disconnected in the dead of another wind-whipped Chicago winter and there was no food, little hope, and no hot water.

The God who held my hand when I witnessed boys in my 'hood swallowed by the elements, by death and by hopelessness; who claimed me when I felt like "no-man's son," amid the absence of any man to wrap his arms around me and tell me, "Everything's going to be okay," to speak proudly of me, to call me son.

I believe in God, God the Father, embodied in his son, Jesus Christ. The God who allowed me to feel His presence—whether by the warmth that filled my belly like hot chocolate on a cold afternoon or that voice, whenever I found myself in the tempest of life's storms, telling me (even when I was told I was "nothing") that I was *something*, that I was His, and that even amid the desertion of the man who gave me his name and DNA and little else, I might find in Him sustenance.

I believe in God, the God whom I have come to know as father, as Abba—Daddy.

I always envied boys I saw walking hand in hand with their fathers. I thirsted for the conversations fathers and sons have about the birds and the bees, or about nothing at all. I longed simply to feel a father's breath, heartbeat, presence. As a boy, I used to sit on the front porch watching the cars roll by, imagining that one day one would park and the man getting out would be *my daddy*. But it never happened.

When I was eighteen, I could find no tears on that Alabama winter's evening in January 1979 as I stood finally—face-to-face—with my father lying cold in a casket, his eyes sealed, his heart no longer beating, his breath forever stilled. Killed in a car accident, he died drunk, leaving me hobbled by the sorrow of years of fatherlessness.

By then, it had been years since Mama had summoned the police to our apartment that night, fearing that Daddy might hurt her—hit her—again. Finally, his alcoholism consumed what good there was of him until it swallowed him whole.

It wasn't until many years later, standing over my father's grave for a long overdue conversation, that my tears flowed. I told him about the man I had become. I told him about how much I wished he had been in my life. And I realized fully that in his absence, I had found another. Or that He—God, the Father, God, my Father—had found me.

My Leading Man

Hamil R. Harris

Los Angeles was still sleeping when I pulled my rented Buick onto the street, away from a squalid one-bedroom apartment in a section of the city called Baldwin Hills. At one time, this community was home to many black actors who lived in posh surroundings high atop the La Brea Mountains. Technically, Dad was in that number, even though his apartment was at the base of a big rock, in a community referred to as "The Jungle."

It was around 4:00 a.m., the air here still cool and the morning sun still not having yet poked through the darkness. By now, the sun surely had already risen miles away above Maryland, where I knew my wife, Taunya, was up and getting my daughter ready for school—shining over the Beltway where people were driving in to Washington, D.C., for work, like I usually did.

But on that midwinter's morning in 1999, I was instead driving this hefty brown-skinned man who was the spitting image of me, but whom I had seen only four other times in my life, to the hospital for a lifesaving medical procedure. Or was I driving him to his grave? The surgical permit he had signed at Cedars-Sinai Medical Center in Beverly Hills covered all the possibilities: angiogram, angioplasty, possible open-heart surgery.

As a man of prayer, I was prepared to send up a heavy petition to God, but my father stopped me abruptly. Dad prayed instead a simple prayer: "Lord, I thank you." With that, an attendant wheeled his gurney into the operating room as I watched them disappear, then returned to a narrow-armed chair in the waiting room where my emotions boiled over quietly.

How can this man hold onto his selfishness to the very end? I thought. How could a man whom I had seen more on a few episodes of *Sanford and Son, Good Times,* and a few other black comedies in the 1960s more than I had seen in the flesh rob me of at least playing the part of the devoted son, of being close to him, of at least getting to know him?

I have always wanted to be close to Henry Harris. I wanted him to know that I loved him, even though I never knew as a little boy whether he loved me. The only information I had about my dad came from my mother, along with the bitterness that too often arises from a failed marriage and divorce—the kind that can cloud any objective assessment of what a father is really like as a human being—before he disappeared from our lives. My mother, Barbara Simmons Harris Rodgers, did a good job of raising me. But in some ways, she deprived me of the chance to know my father. To this day, I have never even seen a photo of my paternal grandmother or grandfather. I don't even know where they are buried.

For most of my life, I had little knowledge of my father, few details of his life and legacy. My mother told me she had escaped in the summer of 1960 while Dad was at the Democratic National Convention, taping speeches of the presidential contenders. He had no idea that when he returned home, that not even a degree from the University of Southern California and his good looks could keep his wife from running far, far away.

For so many years, I was bitter about not having my father in my life. So bitter.

It wasn't until many years later while visiting my father that I began to piece together a portrait of his past, a portrait of who he is, and who, in some ways, I am as his son.

I found the inside of his apartment filled with many contradictions.

One closet held expensive golf clubs, leather bags, and even a few trophies, proof he had clearly taken the game seriously and had relished life. Another closet was filled with shelves of the medicines he has needed for years to stay alive, plagued by diabetes and heart disease.

The carpet in my father's apartment hadn't been cleaned in decades. But inside his closet hung expensive suits he wore to many a casting call. There were boxes and boxes of bills and just as many boxes that contained 8-by-10 photographs, résumés and worn, tattered scripts that belonged to a man who had four decades of movie credits to his name. I found pictures of my dad and Eddie Murphy relaxing around a pool, and other shots from the filming of *Coming to America*. I saw many photos of beautiful young actresses, and also a few unmentionables.

Then I discovered my baby pictures and a newspaper clip from when my mom and dad had gotten married. I found letters, so many letters containing pictures of me and also of my children—letters I had sent— letters that were never completely opened. And yet in all of my discoveries, I found nothing to explain why my father had not sought to close the distance between us.

On that breezy February day in 1999, Henry Harris finally emerged from surgery, a survivor. In some ways, it was the beginning of our new life together, an opportunity to get to know each other, a second chance. Over the next decade, I worked hard to get to know my dad and he worked hard to get to know me. On two different occasions, he has even come to Maryland to visit my wife and children, who now call him "Pop-Pop."

One thing I have learned about him is that my father is committed to the art and craft of the big, and also the little, screen. That for every Charlton Heston or Denzel Washington, there is a Henry Harris. I will never forget the first night I spent in my dad's apartment after he got out of the hospital. He was reciting lines from the different movies he had been in over the years, appearing in minor roles. I was so excited, hanging on every word.

"Man, you have done well as an extra," I suddenly declared.

My father paused, looked at me with raw anger, then shook his head.

"Son, I am not an extra," he scolded. "I am an actor."

Lesson learned.

The last time I traveled to Los Angeles, Dad was well enough to take me to the movies. He chose *No Country for Old Men*. What I found most special about the experience wasn't the movie, but simply being there with my dad and having him share with me the way I always imagined fathers do with sons. And over the last decade, I couldn't have asked much more of Pop-Pop, who tries hard to be in my life, despite his poor health. A few years ago, he suffered a stroke and was found nearly dead in his apartment. He now wears a pacemaker and has had to move out of his apartment into an assisted-living facility in Holly-wood. I am there for him, even though for most of my life, he was not there for me.

I have come to realize that we can spend too much time focused on past events we can't change anyway; that we can only live for now and hope for the future; that the best legacy I can leave for my own son—and daughters—is to be in their lives every day and that it is important for me to try to be the man I want my son to be. I realize that my dad's decision to be a loving father to me, or not, was his to make, and that the decision to be a loving son is mine. I choose love—to forgive and to love.

Not long ago, I was given thirty seconds to accept an Emmy award for a series I helped produce for the *Washington Post*. Standing before the crowd, lights beaming and with tears in my eyes, I dedicated the award to my dad. It just seemed the right thing to do. I choose to see his value in my life, because of the value God has given him by creating him. I can do this now because despite whatever did or didn't happen in the past between him and me, every day I have the opportunity to create legacy and legend. So rather than being angry about what I don't or didn't have, I choose to appreciate what I do have.

I have a father who in the final years of his life has given me mem-ories sufficient enough for a lifetime. I have a father who gives me more than money, credit cards, and bling-bling—a father who, finally, has given me his heart.

Dad calls regularly now. Every time, he asks about my girls, Aria, Alicia, and Alana, and my son, Isaiah, whom he calls "The Prophet."

We don't always get second chances. I am grateful for them and for a God who gives second chances and also strength. And I realize that despite the past sins or shortcomings of my father, and even my own, that in the eyes of my own children, I am their leading man.

HAMIL R. HARRIS—An awarding-winning journalist and author, he has worked at the *Washington Post* since 1992. During his career, Harris has chronicled the political comeback of D.C. mayor Marion Barry, the Million Man March, the Clinton White House, the September 11 attacks, the D.C. Sniper attacks, and Hurricane Katrina. In 2006, Harris was on a team of *Post* reporters that published the newspaper's series *Being a Black Man,* for which Harris won two Emmys, the Casey Medal, and the Peabody Award. He grew up in Pensacola, Florida.

Open Letters to Young Black Men: A Plea for Life

John W. Fountain

As a former Chicago crime reporter, I still carry in my black leather portfolio the reprint of the Tribune's 1993 "Killing Our Children" series of which I took part. The pages are yellowed and tattered now, though the faces of slain children remain vibrant, even if frozen in time in my mind. And though I have long since let my reporter's burden down—the slaying of the young and innocent, keeps happening. But there is no national sense of urgency and no end in sight, only tears. Most of the victims are black and most are murdered by young black men.

These letters were written and published as columns in the Chicago Sun-Times—as pleas to stop the killing.

Stop the Killing

Dear young black man,

They used to come for us cloaked in white sheets and hoods under the cover of night. Today they come in black hoodies and ski masks, by day and by night.

They used to carry our boys away from home, never to be seen alive again. They used to string us up until we dangled like strange fruit from poplar trees, dumped our bodies in murky rivers, or beat us in lynch mobs beyond recognition by our own mothers.

Today, they carry us away in the trunks of cars, leave our young, strong and promising sons, brothers and fathers riddled with bullets, lying naked near railroad tracks, in alleys or fields. They come for us by murderous mob, gun down our young as they play outside. They even shoot our mothers, daughters at bus stops and our babies as they sit innocently in strollers.

Today, the carnage of their homicidal rampage has left an almost endless trail of bodies and blood-stained streets.

Except *they* used to be the Ku Klux Klan.

But today, *they* is you. Oh, young black man.

The Tuskegee Institute in Alabama recorded 3,446 lynchings of blacks from 1882 to 1968—the toll of 86 years. The toll of blacks murdered in Chicago alone over 18 years, from 1991 to 2009: nearly 9,500, and counting.

The numbers alone say you have put the Klan to shame in the killing of African Americans and the terrorizing of black communities. There is no other way to put it: You have become our—your—worst enemy.

It is not by any means the majority of you who are responsible for this fratricide that causes hearse wheels to roll through our neighborhoods like the wind blows.

There are many young brothers striving to keep the faith, living according to the law, seeking to give more than they take—good, promising young men. My letter is not to you but to those who on the surface look like you—those who have allowed evil and hatred to transform them into predators.

Dear brother, as a human being, it is a difficult tragedy to behold. As a black man—as a father—it is sometimes even more than I can bear.

So I write to you, amid news of the slaying of 13-year-old Robert Freeman shot 13 times while riding his bike, and on the heels of nine people shot at a bus stop. I write even as the dust settles upon the graves of the latest homicide victims, and in the midst of a long, hot and bloody summer in which the death bell will toll and toll again before its end.

So why am I writing?

I am writing because statistics show that you most often are our killers. Because young brothers involved in gangs, armed with guns, brazen and filled with rage and having no regard for human life, are responsible for the gunfire that has transformed neighborhoods across America into terror zones fueled by urban tribal wars.

I write to you in the hope that, contrary to popular opinion, some of you do read, in the hope that you might hear the plea of one whose cries reflect the agony of a nation.

So I beg you: Lay down your guns, for the sake of the children, for the sake of our people.

I write to tell you that real power is not in the taking of life but in the giving of life; to inform you that murder is pure evil; and also to share this truth: He that lives by the sword will surely die by the sword, and he who takes a life unjustly will surely have to answer—in this life, or in the next.

It isn't the white man who is making our dear mothers cry. It's you, young black man. And why?

How many of us have to die?

Signed with tears, your brother John.

Hold on to Hope

Dear young black man,

You are a prince, descendant of ancestors who survived the humid hell of slave dungeons and the unforgiving sun of southern plantations, whips and chains, castration, pain.

And even if you never knew the man whose seed you are—that man who was supposed to be your father—you are more than a mistake or statistic. You are life, blood and soul.

You are wondrously made by the creator in the image of Him who has a plan and a good destiny for your life.

And yet, I stood a few days ago inside the Destiny Worship Center on the West Side, the sanctuary filled with teenagers—some wearing memorial T-shirts and a shiny mahogany, rose-draped casket that bore Robert Freeman's 13-year-old body. I stood unable to reconcile the truth with the facts.

The fact is, Robert is dead, shot 13 times, one piercing bullet for each year of life.

The truth is, he shouldn't be.

The fact is, Robert's killer was likely a young black man. The fact is that after my plea to you last week to put down your guns, I was greeted by news the following day of 17 people shot overnight, two fatally, and on Sunday morning to news of 15 more people wounded in overnight shootings, one fatally. Even as I write, is the fact that Tanaja Stokes, 8, is dead—fatally shot in a crossfire while she jumped rope with her cousin Ariana Jones, 7, who was critically wounded.

And the truth, the sad truth, is that unless you stop, the killing of us, this self-inflicted destruction will continue.

Perhaps I am misguided in thinking that my words—an earnest plea in a big-city newspaper—just might reach some of you. Indeed some readers critical of my letter last week contended that you don't read. Some say there is no reasoning with you, that you are a hopeless cause beyond redemption, unreachable.

Not that long ago, they might have said the same of me—black, male and poor, a child of the West Side's North Lawndale—among America's poorest and a member of the "permanent underclass."

Incessant was the sound of gunfire, constant the presence of gangs and crime, the antagonizing memory of an alcoholic father who gave me his name and DNA but little else. Constant was my fear that this might be all there was to life, that I was destined to live and die with the world never having known I existed.

Often my struggle was to hold tightly onto hope like a life preserver when I felt like I was drowning.

What saved me was the understanding that to lose hope was to already have lost the battle. What saved me was choosing to place my faith in something bigger than myself and my circumstances.

What saved me was clinging to something more precious than a big car with shiny rims, fast cash, or the lure of a life as a "baller," sipping cognac with my pick of fine women—big pimpin'.

It was the truth that a man's wealth consists not in the abundance of things he possesses; the truth that there are worse things than dying poor—among them, dealing drugs to my people or contributing even one ounce to their death and destruction; and the truth that if I should gain the whole world and lose my soul, then I would have lost it all.

As they carried Robert's casket out, a scene I have witnessed more times than I can remember over the last 18 years as a journalist—as a black man—there was for me a familiar pain, though incomparable to the agony of Robert's parents who on a sunny summer day had to bury their young prince.

So again I cry, even as Tanaja's parents prepare to bury their little princess: Stop the killing. Stop.

An Open Letter to a Troubled Young Man: Lessons on Manhood

John W. Fountain

This is a real letter, written in response to a note from a young man grappling with the issues of life and seeking to mend his ways and to carve out a new path, despite a sometimes troubled past. The names have been changed.

Hey Jamal:

How are you? I hope things are going well. I meant to write to you before now, but I have been extremely busy with work and with traveling. Even now, I am flying back to Chicago from Atlanta where I was speaking this weekend. I have been up since 4:15 Chicago time and have been averaging about five hours sleep a night for a few weeks now. I'm glad the semester is ending and am looking forward to the summer.

I was glad to hear that everything went well at home and to know that you made it back North with your determination to succeed still intact. I know it's difficult to go home and to see so many people, so many things that you are powerless to change, especially when there are people whom you love who seem trapped in situations. Just remember that in order to help someone we must first put ourselves in a position to help ourselves. That is easier said than done, I know, especially when it seems that there just ought to be something that we should be able to do to help, particularly when it comes to bad situations and circumstances with our mothers. No son wants to see his mother suffer. Just know that God is ultimately in control, and commit your mother, your family, your hopes and dreams to His hands. What I mean by that is, trust God to direct your life, to lead you to the places that He wants you to be, to open the doors that He wants open for you and to close those doors that would lead you down the path of harm.

I remember well what it was like to be sixteen, wondering if I would ever escape my neighborhood in Chicago where poverty, crime and hard times were plenteous, wondering what my life would look like when I was thirty, feeling sometimes like no one really cared about me or believed in me, looking at some of my friends who seemed to have so many more things than I did and who seemed so much better off. There were times that I still felt ashamed, times when I felt like I didn't belong, times when I was angry about my situation, times when I hated my life, times when I thought, *God, you couldn't really love me, or else I wouldn't be here.* Times when I was scared and never told anyone.

All I can tell you is that *feelings* pass, situations change and that even a kid who couldn't afford a five-cent cookie can rise beyond his own dreams, if he's willing to work hard and keeps God as his central focus. I'm not saying that it isn't going to be hard. But it can be done. As my grandmother would say, *I am a living witness.*

Jamal, you have shown that you want to succeed, that you want to change your life, that you want a better life for you and your family. And I think it's safe to say there are people who believe in you and who are rooting for you, among them me. And while I am really glad to see that you have taken hold of the opportunity that Jim and his family have given to you, I am also worried about you, in the sense that I know how difficult it can be to break the cycle, to break away from people you love, but who also seem to suck the life out of you, so that by the time you are done helping them you really have nothing left for yourself. Or you simply are driven—the things you do and the choices you make—by your desire to please or help others. It's like the Chris Rock character in *New Jack City,* the crackhead, who said he was trying to quit, "but it just keeps calling my naaame." *(Okay, you're supposed to laugh at that part.)*

So as much as you are on a new path, it is important for you to understand that there is still so much ground to cover. As much of the past you already have put behind you, it is important to understand that there is still so much that you must forget—so many mountains still to climb. This is important because it can be so easy to begin to feel that everything is now okay, so easy to lose focus and to stop working as hard, to stop being as diligent in your pursuit of changing your life. Home and memories of home, as well as the loved ones we left behind can have a strong draw on us. In other words, they can work like magnets, pulling us almost against our will. I have seen young men and young women who were not able to break away, who, for one reason or another, kept going back, until they were completely consumed.

Jamal, the road ahead will be tough. But the good news is: You can overcome. I did and others have. *You can.* But it will be with hard work, determination, patience and will. It will also take trust. You will have to trust people who you know have your best interest at heart, despite your own mountain of past hurts and disappointments by people in your life who you should have been able to count on, but who failed you—something which makes it hard now for you to trust anyone. I know. I've been there and it ain't easy. But learning to trust is so necessary to you learning to live and ultimately having a better life. *What do I mean by trust?*

I mean relying on someone else's wisdom and experience, someone who has proven they love you. Then you must believe them, even when you can't see the benefits of their wisdom. You must believe that their advice and counsel is good for you and will lead you to a good end.

I have to tell you that the greatest enemy I have ever encountered was not the drug dealers or gangbangers I knew growing up on Chicago's West Side. It was not the white cops who harassed young black men. It was not racism or hate or discrimination. Do you know who my greatest enemy was, what my greatest hurdle was? It was me.

I know that might sound crazy. But my mama used to tell me when I was growing up that our greatest issues are within us. That most of our problems are from within. That try as you may, you cannot run from yourself. My grandmother used to say, "Instead of pointing the finger, point the thumb." Michael Jackson put it this way: "I'm starting with the man in the mirror." *(Okay, laugh again. Man has he got troubles these days.)*

The point is this: People hurt us, they disappoint us, they let us down, they hurt us again. Fathers sometimes aren't around, mothers sometimes can't seem to get off the ground, real friends seem hard to find and the pain of a million lifetimes fills our hearts and minds. But how we choose to react, how we choose to live, whether we choose to be victims or to be molded into abusers, or to drink or smoke our troubles away, is our choice. We can choose life. We have the power to choose life over death.

You have chosen life. And that's a step in the right direction. But each day now, for the rest of your life, Jamal, you must choose life. *Keep choosing life.*

I know, I'm long-winded, but I owe you a few notes. So by the time you read this and chew on it, I should be free of my teaching and all for the summer, so we can talk more frequently. Anyway, there are a few things that really helped me in my journey and which I would like to pass on to you:

Read the Bible
You are what you eat. Garbage in, garbage out.

A daily diet of songs like 50 Cent's "Candy Shop" and other music that has no redeeming value, that emphasizes materialism, sex and thug life won't feed your soul. You're looking for peace and prosperity, for long life and goodness, for inspiration and help for your journey. God's word is fuel for your soul. Start by memorizing Psalm 1. Recite it. Embrace it. Believe it.

Obey Your Parents and Honor Them
Respect is reciprocal. You get back what you give.

The law of the harvest is that a man reaps what he sows. What you give comes back to you. Parents are people, too, and it blesses them when their children respect them. You respect your parents by doing what they tell you to do. And they tell you what to do because they love you. It grieves parents when you complain and talk back, either with your words or by your actions or body language. Love is an action word. Show them your love by obeying, even when it doesn't make sense to you. Their rules are their rules, and children have no right to change or bend those rules. Like God's law, those rules exist for your good, and for the purpose of order. For long life, God says honor your parents. For some, parents are the biological beings who birthed them. For others, parents are those surrogate, and no less loving individuals, whom God has placed in our lives. To dishonor them is to dishonor God.

Work
Real men work. Working is the duty of a real man.

Responsibility is the only thing that distinguishes merely being a male from being a man. The Bible says that whatever we do, we should do as unto God, as if we are working for God himself. God expects and accepts no less than our best. And the process of giving your best, of learning to work hard—to work even in those times when you feel like giving up, when it is hard and you are tempted to quit—is invaluable. It will win the respect of men and will bless you and those around you.

Keep Good Company
Birds of a feather really do flock together. Show me a man's friends and I'll show you the man.

The Bible says that evil communications corrupt good manners, meaning hanging with the homeboys will mess you up. Drug dealers hang with drug dealers; pimps hang with pimps; lions hang with lions; and sheep with sheep. What would happen if a lamb started hanging around lions? It wouldn't be long before he'd become a lamb chop. Find like-minded people. Don't dismiss possible friends because they don't look cool, dress cool or act cool—as in cool by definition of what many young people commonly consider to be cool. Nerds rule the world. And the things we think are cool as kids actually turn out to lead many down the path of a not-so-cool end. Be an individual, a leader, not a follower. Stand up for right. Accept and embrace the good friends that God brings into your life.

Be Humble
Nobody likes a braggart. You can draw more flies with sugar than salt.

The Bible says that if we humble ourselves under the mighty hand of God, He will exalt us in due time; that we ought not think ourselves to be greater than we are. Let your actions speak for you. Be a doer not a talker. Keep your word if you make a promise, knowing that the word of a real man is golden and that once you have lost the respect of others it is hard to get it back. That does not mean that we won't ever make mistakes. Man, I wish. But when we make mistakes, we must ask for forgiveness, understanding that we may not be forgiven, that receiving forgiveness from people we have harmed is not our right, but something that we humbly seek. Manhood is not measured by our brute strength, muscle and courage to face enemies, but often by our ability as men to be tender, to be loving, to be vulnerable, to walk humbly, to walk away when we might be right to physically fight. Our strength as men is measured as much by our ability and willingness to say, "I'm sorry"—by our willingness to walk humbly with God.

Well, Jamal, I pray that you find strength and help in these words. And I hope that before too long we can all get together. By the way, I'm working on my basketball game. I should say that I am running and working out in the weight room, trying to get my legs back. That way when we play a game or two, I can spot you a few points and whip you up. I know that sounds a little like bragging, and after what I said about being humble, it sounds like I'm breaking my own rule. But somebody said, "It ain't bragging if you can do it."

Take care, my brother. Peace and Blessings,

John

Strictly My Father

Teresa Sewell

I was twelve when I realized my father wasn't invincible. The half-inch tube running up his nose and down his throat quieted the thunderous voice that had fussed at me just weeks earlier. The swift-footed man who once hopped out of bed, grabbed his gun, and yelled, "Freeze," to the intruders at our garage door, now lay still in a Holy Cross Hospital bed, worn out from eight days of tests.

I watched as my mother leaned close to him and tried to make out his slow, inarticulate conversation. She spotted me at the door and smiled, but the dimness in her eyes revealed the true vibe of her spirit. The doctors still couldn't explain why his body constantly overheated and bled so profusely from the rectum that he needed a blood transfusion. And after constantly hearing the machines beep like in an *ER* episode, I suddenly realized something: My father might die. That's when regret hit my heart.

For the last few months, I had cursed him with my adolescent mouth and wished I had a better father—one who would hang out with me on Saturdays, praise me for my achievements, and stop zeroing in on my faults.

"No more phone calls for you," he had scolded, "until these boys stop calling here."

My father had his rules. My four sisters and I couldn't date or have male friends until we graduated from high school. Of course, we took that as "we just couldn't let Daddy know about the boys in our lives." At ages twelve, thirteen, and fourteen, our defiance was high, and consequently so was my daddy's anger.

Back then, I didn't see him as being a father trying to keep his family on the right path, only as someone who didn't trust his children because he didn't really know them. In some ways, he really didn't have the time to get to know us. I often watched him come home from work as housing security officer with just enough time to change uniforms, kiss my mother good-bye, and hurry out the door, headed to a side part-time job securing a shopping center or Metra train. He had nine children, and six of us lived with him. And he had to provide for us all. Years later, I would hear him explain, "Y'all had to eat, so I did what I had to do."

But what he had to do eventually disconnected him from his children and us from our father. He was so dedicated to providing the physical necessities that he sometimes forgot the other stuff, the time spent making moments together that little girls and boys carry to adulthood and that last a lifetime—the simple tender memories that can bring smiles to their faces and stir melodies in their hearts.

For six years, my daddy usually worked the 4:00 to 12:00 p.m. shift as a Chicago Housing Authority officer. In the summer, we'd wait up for him every night. And at the point where "J.J." got in his usual trouble on *Good Times*, we'd hear his key turn in the lock.

"Daaaaaddeeee!" we'd yell in unison.

But we were so busy trying to get the Fudge Rounds and Lemonheads out of his hands that we didn't see the heavy burdens he also carried home. Once I remember him stepping only halfway in the door because he had blood on his shoes. He explained that a teenage boy had begged him for help after his leg was nearly sliced off in an argument over a Sega Genesis. Until then, I hadn't realized the danger he was in patrolling the streets of Cabrini-Green and other Chicago housing projects notorious for gangs, drug dealing, shootings, and assorted crime. Daddy came home every night with goodies. So to a child's eye, life was good. It must've been good.

While the strain on my daddy wasn't always apparent, it wore on his body. I didn't know what an ulcer was, but it usually drove Daddy to drink some white stuff called Maalox. I would eventually realize that a main reason Daddy was sick was because he had worked so hard for others, especially his family. My mom was a stay-at-home mom, so Daddy's check was our only source of income.

Every Christmas season, "Up on the Rooftop" would come on the radio and my father would always say, "I remember when you sang that song in kindergarten." When he said this I sometimes grew upset because it was probably the only memory he had of my school assemblies, the only one he had ever attended. "Up on the rooftop," I sang as I pointed my five-year-old finger to the sky with my classmates, "click, click, click / Down through the chimney with Good Saint Nick."

When I walked off the stage, my daddy hugged me like I had just sung for the president. But as I grew older, he was rarely ever there for those special occasions. Not when I was inducted into the National Honor Society. Not when I won the school's spelling bee. In the fifth grade, my teacher Ms. Burden nudged me out of my shell on the day I was supposed to give a speech for student body president. At four feet tall, I couldn't reach the microphone. The crowd giggled and my seventh- and eighth-grade competitors snickered behind me. I went forward anyway, simply saying the speech the way Ms. Burden and I rehearsed. Then suddenly, midway through, the auditorium of more than 500 students stood up and applauded.

"Sewell!" Ms. Burden said as she hugged me. "I knew you could do it, but I didn't know you could do it like that!"

"I wish your parents would've been here."

"Yeah, me too," I said.

My mother, old-fashioned to the core, rarely went anywhere without my father. So that canceled her out for all events too. Back then, this all added up to one thing—my daddy didn't care.

By the time I hit sixth grade, my father had become a police officer and his shift eventually changed to mornings. But instead of running to the door when 4:30 rolled around, we were outside on our bikes trying to avoid him coming home from work. If Daddy saw us with a boy, even if it was one of our neighbors, he'd pull over his blue-and-white '91 Chevy van and force us inside. So we began to hide our friends, our whereabouts, and essentially everything else from him. In doing so, he became less and less my father, and instead someone I had to strategically disobey in order to enjoy life. That was the way I saw it, at least.

But nowadays, at age twenty-four, I sometimes look at my Englewood neighborhood and think about the girls, many of them uneducated, with multiple children by multiple men, or in relationships with men who engage in criminal activity, or who are simply irresponsible. I wonder how the Sewell children would have turned out if my father had been any different. Only two of the nine of us didn't attend college, three have master's degrees, and all of us either have successful careers or are on a clear path toward them. I realize now that maybe my father wasn't the father we sometimes thought he should've been, but it's because of who he is that we are the people we are today.

I see his strength in my sister San, who works 4:00 p.m. to 2:00 a.m., as a hotel supervisor to support her ten-year-old son. I see his willpower in my sister Alicia, who raised a four-year-old child, became a wife, and graduated with a master's while working full-time at age twenty-five.

I can't help but wonder if my sister Laverne would have the compassion to be a high school dean on Chicago's West Side if she hadn't seen my father serve others. I doubt that my brother Darnell could have risen above friends in Englewood and avoided gang life if Daddy hadn't been there.

I don't believe my sister Tiffany would likely see the good in those secluded by others if she had not witnessed that my father's heart was sometimes misjudged as well. William, Jr. wouldn't spend time with Daddy as an adult if in reality he was so bad. My brother Greg wouldn't drive six hours from Ohio just to visit. And perhaps my brother Brian wouldn't invest so much time with his three-year-old son if he hadn't learned from Daddy's mistakes.

Of this much I am sure: I wouldn't write these words if I didn't think there were some fathers who are sometimes so misunderstood by their own children. And this much I have resolved: That even if I was angry at all the things he didn't do, I owed him honor for everything he did.

That hospital bed helped me to begin to see that.

We eventually transferred my father to Michael Reese Hospital. Within a week, doctors diagnosed him with diverticulitis—an ailment that affects the large intestine—and he had surgery. By day fifteen, Daddy was home.

There were still difficult times throughout the years. In fact, most of my revelation didn't come until adulthood. There is one memory in particular. I was twenty and my father had driven two hours to the University of Illinois at Urbana-Champaign for an awards ceremony where I was being honored. Afterward, my parents dropped me off at my dorm.

"Thanks for coming," I said, then walked toward my residence hall. Then I heard my father call my name. "Teresa," he yelled. I turned around. Then the words fell from his lips to my heart. "We're proud of you," he said from the car. "Keep it up."

"Thanks," I said with a smile and waved good-bye.

The five-page paper I had due the next day had been on my mind all morning long. But for a moment, I no longer cared. I had a song in my heart:

"Up on the rooftop / click, click, click," I sang. "Down through the chimney / with Good Saint Nick."

TERESA SEWELL—A native of Chicago's South Side, she knew she was destined to become a journalist when in high school she reported on the shooting death of a fellow classmate at Chicago Vocational Career Academy. Teresa earned a bachelor's degree in news-editorial journalism at the University of Illinois at Urbana-Champaign. She has worked as a reporter-intern at the *State Journal-Register* in Springfield, Illinois, and the *Chicago Sun-Times*. She is a recent graduate of the Medill School of Journalism at Northwestern University, where she earned a master's in broadcast journalism and recently started a documentary company called OverFlo Produxions.

Never Too Late

Sylvester Monroe

San Francisco (June 2000)

As baseball games go, the San Francisco Giants' 18–0 rout of the Montreal Expos at Pac Bell Park last month was about as good as the national pastime gets. Barry Bonds splashed a homer in the big pond, and even the pitcher hit a grand slam. But as great as the game was, the feats on the field paled in comparison to what went on in the stands. That was the first and only baseball game I have ever been to with my father.

I grew up believing my father had been lost and presumed killed in the Korean War. When my maternal grandfather wouldn't let him marry my pregnant mother, a high school senior at the time, the nineteen-year-old prospective father joined the air force and landed in Korea just months after I was born.

Soon after that, my mother also left their Mississippi Delta hometown and headed north to Chicago. For a while, she stayed in touch with my father's family, but after a time she lost touch with them completely. Except for my mother's memories, all I had of my father was a 5-by-7 sepia-tone photo of him in his air force uniform and another snapshot of him in his high school football jersey, No. 33. I wore that number during my own short-lived high school football career.

Call of a Lifetime

I was a twenty-two-year-old cub reporter at *Newsweek* magazine in Boston when, out of the blue, I got an amazing telephone call from my mother in Chicago. "Are you sitting down?" she began.

"I just ran into your father's sister. She says he is alive and living in Northern California. He's been there for the last twenty-some years. Tried to find us, but didn't know where we were."

It is difficult to describe what I felt at that moment. I did not whoop and holler. I did not cry. I did not do or think anything. I simply tried to comprehend the true meaning of the revelation: Your father is alive. It wasn't easy.

The thing I'd dreamed, talked, and thought about all my life was a reality. My father—Kittrel D. Peoples—was alive and well. Still, it was weeks before I could even pick up the telephone to call him. What would I say? What would he say? What if I didn't like him? What if he didn't like me? As happy as I wanted to be, I was also afraid that meeting the real man might tarnish the spit-and-polished war hero image I'd carried of my dad for so many years.

After an awkward first coast-to-coast long-distance phone call, we did talk from time to time. But it was six more years before we finally met. It happened at my dad's oldest brother's home in Richmond during 1979, when I was on a journalism fellowship at Stanford University. After a huge bear hug from this stranger who looked like an older, darker version of myself, we sat down to find common ground.

"Why don't we get out of here and go get a beer?" he asked, trying to break the ice.

"I don't like beer," I replied, almost instantly regretting that out of nervousness I hadn't taken the offer anyway.

"Can you drive a truck?" he asked.

"Sure."

"Let's take a ride," he said, oddly enthusiastic.

We walked outside to the curb, where an old, beat-up pickup truck sat. I slid behind the wheel, turned the key, and stepped on the gas. The truck jumped off like a jet. "Wow!" I said, feeling the power of the souped-up engine.

"You like my truck?" he asked quietly.

"Yeah, man, it's great," I said.

"Good, he said happily. "I always wanted my son to drive my truck."

A Beautiful Friendship

That was the true beginning of a friendship that blossomed over two decades in ways I could never have imagined. Each time I talk to my father I learn something new and fascinating about who I am and where I come from and why I like certain things. As his only natural child, I have mannerisms I share with him. For example, when I'm deep in thought, I habitually twirl my thumbs and so does he. In fact, Jason, who is my only son, does the same thing.

I thought of such things as I watched the Elian Gonzalez saga. For me, that Elian should be with his father was a no-brainer. To needlessly separate the boy from his father would have been the real crime. Sure, Elian could have had a wonderful life with his Miami relatives, just as my life was far from horrible without my father.

In fact, though I did not have him to take me to baseball games and father-son events, my mother's five brothers and her father stepped up as super surrogates.

One taught me to hit a baseball and how to play shortstop. He watched me play Little League and took me to major league games. Another taught me practically everything I know about cars, including how to drive. He even loaned me his car before I was old enough to have my own. Still another came with my mother to my high school and college graduations. My grandfather told me wonderful tales, some taller than others, that inspired me and nurtured my own desire to become a storyteller.

In short, they helped my mother provide the love, support, and sense of self-worth that are the basic currency of healthy and happy childhood development. Though poor and largely fatherless, I was never deprived in the "feeling loved" department.

But still, it was not the same as having my father there to do all those things with me. Through my childhood, I quietly envied the kids who had that.

Depending on Mother

Growing up without a father tends to make a boy (or girl, and make no mistake about it, daughters need their fathers as much as sons) more dependent upon his mother. I learned I could always depend on my mother, no matter what. I grew up trying not to emulate many of the men I saw around me–from absentee fathers to abusive and "trifling" husbands.

My late stepfather, who was in and mostly out of my life from the time I was six until I went away to boarding school at fourteen, was such a person. Though I loved him dearly and thought he was the coolest man I had ever known, his repeated broken promises made an imprint on my psyche. Once, when I was eight, he promised to take me to a Harlem Globetrotters game. For a full week, all I could think about was going to that game with him.

The night before, I couldn't sleep at all. As the time approached, I waited in the front window for his car to drive up. The game was to start at 8:00 p.m., and he said he'd be there at half past 6:00. When he hadn't arrived by that time, I believed he was just a little late. By 8:30, I was still in the window, unwilling to accept the truth. My mother finally made me go to bed at 9:00, soothing my disappointment as she had so many times before.

Two days later, he showed up as if he'd simply missed a television program. "Hey, Syl," (only he called me that, and I grew to hate it) he began, "Daddy got tied up. I'll make it up to you, though. You still love me, don't you?"

As I had countless times before and would many times after, I said, "Yes," hugged him, and tucked away my disappointment in the secret place where I hid all such pain.

Growing up without a father also makes it difficult to know how to be one. Becoming a father at eighteen, I didn't have a clue about what I was supposed to do. But I did have a pretty good idea of what I should not do. That came in handy years later when I had a difficult promise to keep with my own young son.

During the 1984 presidential campaign when I was on the road working as a reporter for fourteen months straight, I had promised my son I would be in Chicago with him for my birthday. As it turned out, I had the day off, but I was in Boston, not Chicago. I was dead tired, and the thought of getting on an airplane just to have a seven-year-old sing "Happy Birthday" to me was about the last thing I wanted to do. But I remembered the broken promises of my own childhood and dragged myself from Boston to Chicago.

When I arrived, it was past 9:00 p.m. and Jason was already asleep. His mother, Regina, gave me an earful. "I don't know why you told this boy you were going to be here anyway," she snapped. "You know how busy you are. He's been out on that balcony all day waiting for you. Every car that passed that he thought might be you, he'd start shouting. 'That's my daddy, that's my daddy.' He wouldn't eat, and I finally had to make him go to bed. So now I suppose you're going to wake him up."

I definitely did.

And the first thing Jason did was turn to his mother and say, "See, I told you he was coming."

Over the years, I have tried to be the father I always wanted. Above all else, I reasoned that being a dad means being there not just on special occasions, but every day. And sometimes, it means being there even when you need or want to be somewhere else. That is what I love so much about Kittrel D. Peoples, this man I have come to know as my dad. I know he would have been there if he could have.

On Jason's twenty-first birthday, he flew on short notice all the way from San Francisco to Atlanta to celebrate his grandson's coming of age. He didn't have to, and everyone would have understood if he hadn't. But he did. And he did it again for his granddaughter's wedding. And now, as he gets ready to turn sixty-nine in September, he continues to do it whenever I call him.

It's why sitting in Pac Bell Park with him last month made the eight-year-old boy inside the forty-eight-year-old man I am today so blissfully happy to be able to say, "I went to the Giants game with my dad." Thanks, Dad, for being there.

Sylvester Monroe's dad passed away in 2008.

SYLVESTER MONROE—Formerly senior editor of *Ebony* magazine, Monroe is a dec-orated veteran journalist and best-selling author. In his memoir, *Brothers: Black and Poor—A True Story of Courage and Survival,* he chronicles his story of growing up in Chicago's Robert Taylor Homes and his matriculation to Harvard University. A long-time correspondent for *Newsweek* and later for *Time* magazine, he has won numerous awards for his reporting and writing, and over the course of a noted journalism career has covered issues ranging from desegregation to urban poverty and education and politics, including Harold Washington's successful bid to become Chicago's first black mayor and Reverend Jesse Jackson's historic 1984 campaign for president.

I'd Rather Have You

John W. Fountain

I'd rather have your breath
That's real.
Have your touch
Just one day.
To feel
Rather see your face
Again and again with my eyes
Than imagine in my mind.
Rather have you here
Than have to seek to find.
Rather know your foibles
And love you in spite.
Never have to imagine with all my might.
I'd rather know your imperfections
Than be left with my own reflections of the man
I can't see
Can't remember
Can't hear
And each September forget which day
Was the day you were born.

Instead I mourn
The man I never knew.
How much I'd give
How much I'd do
Just once to hear you
Just once to see you
Just once to be with you
To walk again hand in hand
To know and touch the man
Who is my father.

Redemption

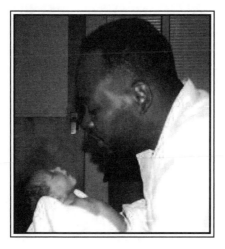

And the Lord thy God will bring thee into the land which
thy fathers possessed, and thou shalt possess it...
Deuteronomy 30:5

John W. Fountain and newborn daughter Imani.

Lip Gloss, Hot Sauce,
and a Father's Loving Thoughts:
An Open Letter to a Daughter

John W. Fountain

On a snowy Virginia morning that November when the flakes were falling like white feathers from the blue sky, your mother lay on the sofa in our living room, the pains of early labor coming and going as I stood with a stopwatch, looking more like a nervous coach than an expectant father, making notes each time. And we knew: It was time. Music filled the room—Bobby Lyle's "Christmas Song"—the sound of soft piano filling the spaces in between your mother's moans from her contractions. And we knew: It was time.

For months, we had been awaiting your arrival. I had painted your bedroom a soft powder blue, bought a giant stuffed bear, and assembled your crib. We had decorated your room with an assortment of stuffed animals and knickknacks and all the accessories for a new baby, including a changing table laden with Pampers and powder. We had even picked out a name: Imani. It was for me a special name. It is Swahili for the word "faith."

I needed faith. Years earlier, I had lost it. It is the kind of thing that sometimes happens to people on the road of life from childhood to adulthood, and even along the road from adulthood to the twilight years of life when we all eventually turn aged and gray and the light of life slowly dims in our eyes. Someone said life is what happens while you're making other plans. And I guess life happened to me. I became a teenage parent. Soon after, I was married with three children, then eventually divorced. I had known poverty as a child, then poverty as an adult. And I had scars from having grown up as a little boy without my natural father. They were not physical scars, the kind that you can rub, touch, soothe, and fade with creams and Vaseline and cocoa butter. But they were scars no less—emotional scars, the kind of scars that do not so easily fade. The scars of rejection. Scars of disappointment. Of fear and hopelessness. I'm talking about the kinds of scars that I never want you to have because of a father's unwillingness to be in your life. So just as we adults sometimes suffer scars as we stumble along the road of life, there are times when we must also find faith if we are to find hope for healing. And that's where you come in.

Truth is, after being a single parent, after years of disappointment as a father myself and the years of disappointment from early childhood as a son, along with all the pressures and challenges of life, I didn't want to have any more children. Not even half of one. Well, that was a bit of a problem, for I had remarried, and the lovely young woman whom I married didn't have any biological children. But I had written her a promise on a napkin at the Denny's restaurant on North Harlem Avenue in Oak Park, Illinois, where we often ate French toast and bacon and eggs when we were just engaged. That promise was that someday, when we were both ready, I would be willing to have a child. That day came. And we planned for you, though we could not have known it would be you or how you would look when you were born, how you would sound someday when you spoke your first words, what your personality might be, or whether you might dislike oatmeal, like your dad, or like the color purple, like your mom. This much we did know: That you would be our little girl. Daddy's little girl. And that alone made you special.

So you needed a special name. Of all the names we considered—Nia, Monique, Sha-nay-nay *(just kidding, smile)*—there was one that seemed perfect. One that captured my hopes for a yet unborn daughter, one that also reflected my decision to try and move beyond the hurts of my own past and to move forward into a future of a brighter tomorrow. That name was Imani.

So we whispered it. From your mom's and my lips to her round belly, from the time after the ultrasound pictures at the doctor's office first showed that the baby she was carrying was a girl, we called you by your name. For months, we called you, sang to you, and dreamed of the day when you would finally be here and we could see your face, hold you, care for you. I even made up a song that I would sing sometimes to your mother's womb and that I would sing to you after you were born as I cradled you in my arms:

Imani, Imani
Precious Little Baby Girl of Faith
Imani, Imani
I can hardly wait to see your face
I-M-A-N-I
You are precious, that is why
Precious Little Baby Girl of Faith

On that morning of November 15, 1995, as the snow fell, and the pains came, and the breath of winter hung in the Virginia air, we knew: It was time.

Shortly after 6:30 p.m. that Wednesday evening, I watched as your mom gave her final push in the room at Alexandria Hospital, and your wet, black, straight hair slicked to your head finally poked through fully into the light of life. I watched as they suctioned you and you took your first breath and cried. I cried, too, at the sight of you, perfect, beautiful, our daughter, my daughter. And every hope I ever had for you, every expectation, every joy a father could ever find in a daughter, I found in you that day, in that moment, in that room.

Almost thirteen years later, I sit here at home in my office on this autumn morning, tapping the keys of my laptop, wondering where the years have gone. It's 7:18 a.m. now, and we are hundreds of miles from Virginia and back in our home state, Illinois. You are upstairs getting ready for school. It's hard to believe you are in the seventh grade, hard to see the metamorphosis taking place before my eyes as you blossom from a little girl into a young woman. You're nearly as tall as your mother, looking more grown up, going to the beauty shop more, wearing lip gloss *(remember: less is more)*, and experiencing changes in your body that signal you are closer to being a woman than you are to that baby whom I dressed in her sweater and booties and carried home two days after she was born. And as I stare face-to-face into this reality, I also face the reality that you have less than the time you have been with us over these last nearly thirteen years to be with us here in our home. That you, in only five years, will be headed off to college. That my baby will be gone.

And yet I find that less difficult to deal with than the fact that the world sometimes can be cold and cruel. And without the protection of fathers, daughters can sometimes find themselves in difficult, if not also perilous situations, particularly with men who love less, care less, and think less of them than their loving fathers.

There is, quite frankly, so much wrong with the world right now. And one of my greatest concerns for you as your father is that, as is the case for so many young women, there is the potential for you to someday meet Mr. Wonderful, who will eventually turn out to be Mr. Horrible. And while no man is perfect, including your father, you are too perfect to ever have to deal with some men's imperfections, which can hold deadly consequences for you, both emotionally and physically. Even as I write this, Chicago is saddened by the news of the slaying of actress and Grammy Award–winner Jennifer Hudson's family. The suspect indicted by a grand jury in the case is the husband of Jennifer Hudson's sister, Julia Hudson, who reportedly was angered over some disagreement with his wife, from whom he was separated. He has been indicted on three counts of homicide in the shooting deaths of Hudson's mother, brother, and her sister's seven-year-old son, and is still awaiting trial.

So many people here in Chicago and across the country and the world were saddened and deeply troubled by the tragedy. And so many wonder why Jennifer Hudson's mother, Darnell Donerson, had not moved out of the Englewood neighborhood where they lived after her daughter Jennifer became rich and famous. Maybe that's another story. But what I cannot clear from my mind are thoughts of so many young women who have grown up with visions of someday finding Mr. Right but ending up with Mr. Wrong, only to discover that they were indeed sleeping with the enemy—that they had connected themselves with pure unadulterated evil.

Oh, these types of men and boys are flesh and blood, all right. But the sum of them—their character, psyche, and moral compasses are warped, twisted, and scarred like the face of Frankenstein's monster. The only problem is "bad" men and boys often don't look like monsters. And they often don't act like monsters. Although like monsters, once they feel that it is safe to come out, they show their true self. Still, I suspect there are always signs.

In any number of cases of which I am aware that for some woman ended in tragedy at the hands of a supposed lover, the man had served time for violent crimes or had been caught dealing drugs, and displayed extremely violent behavior, even the lack of self-control. Yet women sometimes still do not heed these warning signs, feel instead that they can make Mr. Wrong right, love him into being a better man, mold him into the man they want—wish—him to be. But baby, take it from me—a man filled with his own flaws and foibles, and who has had his own shortcomings to overcome and inner demons to subdue and slay—the only one who can change a man is that man, and that with the help of his God. But even God allows that man to make his own choices.

You, as a young woman and an adult woman, will have choices to make, so many critical choices to make, as you find your way along this winding and sometimes treacherous journey called life. And how I wish I could keep you safe, shrink you as I sometimes say, keep you little and carry you, tuck you in at night always and just look in on you while you are sleeping soundly, be able to whisper a prayer as I pull the covers up around your neck and kiss you on the forehead. I wish I could always know where you are, be there within arm's reach, should you ever need me, the same way I did when you lay in an incubator beneath the purplish bili lights hours after you were born because you were jaundiced. But the understanding that at least in some ways I cannot, and the reality that in some ways, even if I could, it would not be good for you—that the time surely comes for us daddies to let our precious daughters go—that lets me know that it is time.

Not time to let go. But time to share some of my truths about life and love and living in an imperfect world filled with men, good and bad, and some who lurk like wolves in the mist for the chance to devour girls—women—like you. I don't mean to scare you. I love you and I want you for all of your days to be filled with joy and happiness. And so, I feel I would be less than a father to not try and steer you away from the potholes and pitfalls, to try and provide you with what I hope will be an eternal safety net, and to provide for you, in those times when you cannot hear my voice, at least my words, words from your father—your first love.

And so, with your birthday a few weeks away, I am embarking upon a little journey to write this book for you. It is a book that I hope will help fortify you against the monsters and also help you to detect them, a book in which you will find some humor at times, and at other times counsel, comfort. At other times, it will serve to remind you who and whose you are and to reassure you that you are never alone. There are thirty chapters in all—short and sweet chapters—meant for you to read as a devotional each corresponding day of the month, and meant to be read again and again as you find the need at various times in your life.

There are secrets in this book. Secrets of men. Secrets of women. Secrets of the brokenhearted. Secrets of the pathway toward healing and the secret to surviving whatever twists and turns or storms and showers life may bring, the secret to remaining unbroken. This book is my gift to you—a gift that I hope you can share over the years with other girls or women, especially those who have no experience or recollection of a father's words. Girls and women whose hearts are broken, who smile on the outside but who cry on the inside from the hurts suffered at the hands of broken or bad men. For the little girl inside those women who have never known the tenderness of a father, and even those for whom a father's platonic touch and soothing reassurance no longer exists and has perhaps faded from memory.

But Imani, this book is also my song to you, a song written for you, my daughter—the little girl who has brought me joy from the moment I first saw her. The little girl who still makes tears fill my eyes, whom I have watched work diligently in school and be kind to others. The girl with the caring heart, who loves Ramen noodles, *That's So Raven*, doing the Cupid Shuffle, dining at Red Lobster, planning for birthdays and holidays and painting her nails. And yes, lip gloss and hot sauce. The girl who makes me proud simply to be her father. This book, this song, is for you.

May its melody forever play in your head, soothe your soul, restore you, renew you, reassure. And should there ever come a time when you are less than sure of yourself, may your father's song remind you, lead back to the irrefutable reflection and revelation of you, to the true essence of you. To the knowledge that you are forever beautiful, perfect, and wondrously made, inasmuch as you were that snowy Virginia day of your birth when I first set my eyes upon you and loved you for just one sufficient reason: Because of who you are.

Where Were You?

Vincent C. Allen

There I stood at the ceremony with my feet at a forty-five-degree angle, my thumbs running along the seams of my trousers, shoulders as erect as the Statue of Liberty, head held high as one who has just been given an opportunity for a promising future in the U.S. Marine Corps. I resisted the urge to look around at the crowd of family and friends in attendance, in part because I feared the fury of the attack I knew I would have encountered from one of those drill instructors who had made their position clear some eleven weeks earlier, but mostly because I knew there was no need to look for "them." I knew "they" were not there. More important, I knew "he" was not there.

Truth is, he had never been there. In fact, at that point in my life, I had only ever seen him once and had clung to that encounter as something I didn't want to ever forget.

For most of my life, my father was MIA.

He seemed to live as though his absence did not affect me. I, however, believe that it did. I know it did. In time, I chalked up his absence as having been his loss. And I accepted as best I could that I likely would never really know the man responsible for my existence. By age nineteen, my father had already missed a lifetime of moments. But why did he miss this moment?

I had just accomplished something the other eighty-five stalwart young men had not. I not only graduated from the eleven-week transformation of the U.S. Marine Corps basic training, but I did so as the number-one recruit for Platoon 1060 in September 1982—crowned the "honor" graduate. But now, who was I going to celebrate with?

It seemed as if every one of the newly christened U.S. Marines had someone to congratulate him. I had no one. No mother. No brothers or sisters. Not an aunt or uncle. No father.

I played it off, at times stone-faced, other times smiling nonchalantly, as if their—as if his—absence did not matter. Years later, I had to recognize it did.

My feelings, I later came to understand, had been pushed to the cellar of my own consciousness and had no reason to reemerge. It was perhaps a disappearing act necessary for my own survival. In fact, I eventually became quite comfortable living as if I did not need a father, or a mother or anyone else. Long before I became a teenager, I had already endured more parental neglect and hurts than I care to remember.

There were times when my stepfather beat and mistreated me; my mother left, leaving me behind to live with my great-aunt. I was punished for not knowing my ABCs. I even failed the first grade. At age five, I fell from a second-floor window onto unforgiving concrete pavement. Later, I was hit by a cab. And finally, three years after my mother had left, I was reunited with her and moved to Detroit for what remained of my formative years, though still without him—without my father or any semblance of a man, someone who might have comforted, consoled, or protected me during those traumatic moments of my early childhood years.

Where was he? I often wondered silently. *What was his reason for not being there? What did I do? Why did I run him away? Why didn't he desire to have a relationship with me?*

In time, the abuse I suffered ended, my wounds eventually healed, and the relationship with my mother was restored. But one stinging question still haunted me throughout my adult life: *Where was he? Who was he?*

Finally Face-to-Face

For much of the early years, I only heard bad things about him. Mostly, my father was a ghost, a figment of my imagination since I had never even seen a picture of him.

I was ten or eleven when I finally got the chance to meet him. That summer day, he walked into the house—standing about five feet ten, to my best recollection, though the image of him has faded with time. Seeing him that day for the very first time did not immediately stir up warm and fuzzy feelings. In fact, "Daddy" was not a thought as I stood watching him walk through our door. It was as if he were simply another man my mother had brought into our house. The only difference was that he entered with a few other people and wore a kind of arrogant expression that I later learned was the spirit of Mr. Wild Irish Rose.

After a few minutes of chitchat, he asked if I would go for a walk with him. I said yes. As we strolled, I thought, "Wow, I'm walking with the man who gave me life." Even as I recall our meeting, now, many years later, deep feelings of nostalgia grip me.

Minutes before we had embarked on that journey of a lifetime, my father had given me the only thing besides my very being that he ever gave me that was tangible: Two dollars. Two bucks in 1975 was a lot of money. So not only did his gift to me make him "amazing" in my eyes, he was rich!

My fairy tale, however, soon disappeared when our long-awaited-for father-and-son stroll ended at a corner liquor store, where my father quickly disappeared, then, like a lightning bolt, reappeared only to ask for the only tangible, worthwhile thing he had ever given me. Having bestowed it just ten minutes earlier, he now wanted it back, though I could never have imagined that my "rich" father from New York had given me his last two dollars. Looking back now, it was like I was sitting at a poker table, plenty of chips on my side and waiting for the river card to give me life because I was all in. Then it happened. Suddenly, my father fired off like a marine drill instructor, giving directions to a bus full of scared lonely boys waiting to become the world's finest fighting machines.

"Let me have the two dollars I gave you," he said without hesitation or remorse. "I will give them back to you later."

Such was our first meeting.

The second time I saw him, I was a decorated marine gunnery sergeant with medals to prove I had not failed. But he could not see them. He could not see me. He was unaware of my presence, unaware that I had four wonderful children and a wife. He could not grasp that I was living in Italy, proving my love for our country and NATO by my service. He could not see the man I had become, nor hear the words of forgiveness I might whisper in his ear.

And as I neared his casket that winter day in 1998, what I also understood was that I would never get my two dollars back, that I could never ask him why he chose to not be in my life or why he had allowed himself to pass from this earthly realm to the afterlife, leaving behind a son still so vexed by his absence, still longing for answers.

Reflections

It is winter now, and my father many years buried. And yet I still wish I could speak to him. I still long for a father-son conversation, the kind I have had with my own two sons, now adults. I desire to share with him that I have never spent time incarcerated. That I have not made mine a life of cheating and abusing my body or others around me.

I long to tell him that I forgive him, to introduce him to my beautiful wife, Felicia, to whom I have been married twenty-four years; to have him meet my four children, Tanisha, Crystal, Vincent, Jr., and Branden; and our three grandchildren, DeShawn, Jalen, and Taiya. I want to tell him how I have turned out to be a preacher and pastor and made a career of the Corps. That I am committed to and involved in bettering people's lives. And that I have chosen to be an asset rather than a liability to society. But, he is not here. He is no longer here.

And so, at forty-six, I remain dubious about why he chose absence over presence. Is it better to have never known, or to have known and lost? What might life have been like with him? Questions and feelings of nostalgia linger. So many questions. At times, they compass me about and entice me to dwell too long on the past and on loss.

But I am imbued with the possibilities of the future. And while I realize now that I will never have all the answers, I have resolved to find solace in the fact that the living God has been a father to the fatherless—and that He has been my father. That Christ Jesus has promised to be with the human family that trusts in Him.

Although I continue to find comfort in His word, it does not eliminate the late-night toil of the little boy inside me who still longs for the experience of an earthly father and who still asks in moments of human frailty and amid the sting of abandonment, "What if?" and "What did I do?"

While I did not find the answers as the abandoned son, I did find them along my mission to be a father who might never do the same to his children.

So although I became a father at age fifteen and had my second daughter by eighteen, I purposed in my mind to not be like my father, even if I did not understand fully what being a good father entailed. My own father's absence caused me to remain faithful to my daughters and to their welfare. So that even though we were not in the same household, and even though my career in the military carried me across the seas, from shore to shore, and into battles and wars, into harm's way often with no assurance that I would return, I did my best to stay connected. At times, I was better than at other times. But I never lost focus, always endeavoring to be their lifeline, to be more than some distant hazy figure in their minds. My father taught me that by his absence. He taught me in ways he will never know.

My children have never known a grandfather. Yet each one of them has had their father all of their lives. That was my purpose as a father, my mission as a man.

Epilogue

I do not know if I am a better man than my father. And perhaps that is not for me to say. What I can say, what I can say assuredly, is that I have striven always—no matter life's innumerable challenges and trials—to be a better father, to carry myself as a moral and responsible man of which my children and my family could be proud. And I can say with as much certainty that my two sons—twenty-one and nineteen—have for their lives observed a man dedicated to them and to their mother. I have attended school events, assemblies, and other activities in which they were involved. And I have tried to impart to them the life lessons that will aid in their personal endeavors as men and also someday as fathers.

Regarding my own father, I know that I still carry many unresolved issues within my heart, which every now and again resurface. But I also know that I must remain steadfast in my belief that my heavenly Father will carry me through those moments of loneliness and longing. This much I also know and have resolved: I do not hate my father. And I am grateful to him and my mother for bringing me into this world, for giving me life.

But as a grandfather of two bright young men and one gregarious young lady, I am deliberate in giving them memories, enough to share with their children and their children's children—memories enough for a lifetime, memories of me being there.

VINCENT ALLEN—Pastor and founder of Agape Fellowship Ministries in Stafford, Virginia, he is a native of Detroit, Michigan, and a retired U.S. Marine who served more than two decades in service to his country, working over the course of his career on all levels of administration, including as administrative chief for two former assistant commandants of the U.S. Marine Corps. He also served in Naples, Italy, with Allied Forces, Southern Europe, where he founded a ministry serving both Italians and Americans. He currently pastors in Stafford, Virginia.

Absent but Always Present

Monica Fountain

My father never went on a school field trip. Never came to a football or basketball game where I was shaking my pom-poms in what he still jokingly describes as my little "bobtail skirt." He didn't attend the school musical or the play I wrote in high school. When he did come to the school, he usually wasn't there for me.

Instead, he was helping a single mother get her wayward son back in school. Or he was fighting the local powers that be, protesting to get more black teachers hired for a school enrollment that was increasingly black and a school staff that was stubbornly white. He was often marching off to school board meetings or rallies and organizing the community for another civil fight. Or he was protesting the number of black boys being expelled and suspended—my father's days and nights filled with meetings and causes and prayer.

My mother was the one who registered me and my brother, Ed, for school. The one who was there for parent-teacher conferences and field trips. She was the one in attendance on Senior Night at football and basketball games, though like my father, she also sometimes stood in as parent for some child at church or one whom she knew from our small-town community.

I shared my parents, especially my father. He had scores of sons and daughters, though in actuality my mother gave birth to just two: Ed and me—six years younger. We were PKs, preacher's kids. My father was pastor of the Morning Star Missionary Baptist Church, the largest African American church in Kankakee, Illinois, our town of 30,000— and arguably the most influential church. It was largely my dad—the Reverend William H. Copeland, Jr.—who made it so, a caramel-complected slender man whose politics and hands-on liberation theology were shaped in a Jim Crow Louisiana and in the faith of his father, himself a Methodist preacher.

Dad had a sometimes raspy voice that when he stood in the pulpit on Sunday mornings, when it was buttered with the spirit, thundered as he preached. It was the same fire of righteous indignation that I later recall hearing in his voice when there was some injustice he sensed, some new cause to battle, some compulsion or call to help someone in need.

And so his presence in one place meant his absence in another. Such is the calling of a preacher, and also the burden of being a natural-born PK.

The Real Thing

I can't say that I knew where my father was when I was singing "Oklahoma," back in high school or even as a pom-pom girl that time when the batteries went dead on the tape player during a dance routine—and "you dropped the bomb onnnnn meeeeee" suddenly fizzled across the gymnasium—creating one of my life's most embarrassing moments. I just knew he wasn't there and that I don't really remember expecting him to be there, though with my mother ever present, I never remember feeling deprived by Dad's absence.

Dad's job was to help others. That much I understood, even as a child.

For thirty-six years, my father was the pastor of Morning Star.

He often tells a story, probably too often for those at the church who had to hear it every time I have been in attendance at service. It is the story of me being his only "real daughter." The story goes: One day he was calling some of the girls in the congregation "daughter" as he usually did, and on that particular day I told a visiting minister, "He calls them daughter, but I'm the only real daughter he has."

It was not a strange thing for me, sharing my father with the world. But I guess there was a part of me that at times wanted to assert that I was the real thing. The One and Only. The Truth.

I have wondered if Dr. Martin Luther King, Jr.'s children ever felt that way. Was their father a figure who passed in and out of their lives? Did he make time to make special memories with them? Did they understand their father didn't just belong to them, but to the world? I wonder if his little girls ever felt like saying sometimes, "I'm the real thing."

Having to share my father was not a constant abrasive. It was simply the way it was. My father happened to be the pastor, though I later discovered that most people didn't understand what being a pastor really meant.

My god-sister and god-brother once asked me what my father's job was. They thought he only preached on Sunday mornings. They hadn't a clue that he also went to the church almost every day of the week, answered calls for help in the middle of the night, counseled couples whose marriages were on the brink of divorce, visited the sick in the hospital, taught Bible classes, and handled the business of the church, which was ever constant.

They didn't understand that in my father's eyes and in ours, "the church" went beyond what happened within its walls but extended to what happened in people's everyday lives.

So Dad went to the school. He went to factories and protested when workers believed they were unjustly fired. He marched in the street against gang violence and met with gang members to negotiate a truce. He founded the local chapter of the NAACP after a mother called him about an incident involving her daughter: The young woman was working at a fast-food restaurant and her white manager had kicked her in her posterior. My father went to the restaurant every day looking for the manager. Ultimately, he scared that man straight and the white manager pleaded for her forgiveness. So the story goes.

The demand for my father's time was never ending. Once, police called him when a man was locked in his car on the nearby interstate and threatening to shoot himself. Dad went to the scene and convinced the man to come out peacefully.

But inasmuch as my father gave of himself, his sacrifice was not always embraced. And inasmuch as his critics' cruelty cut him, it also hurt me—us—though in all of his hurt, even at the hands of some of those whom he loved and with whom he had fellowshipped and even mentored, he never relented in his faith and calling. He never gave in, even as he was talked about and maligned, followed by the police, our telephones tapped, betrayed by some and backstabbed by others whom he would turn around and help again when they incurred new troubles and their pressing needs stole more of our time with him.

Roots

We did share father-daughter moments. I cherish them.

Once, my father took me fishing. I couldn't have been more than seven. We cast our fishing poles in glistening waters on a sun-scorched day—a day on which I caught the biggest fish but almost fell into the river. Dad's strong hands pulled me back.

Once, when my mother had to go out of town to care for her ailing father, my father did my hair. He had plaited my hair in a bunch of little braids that stuck out in every which way, making me look like Kizzy from *Roots*. I looked in the mirror and cried. "I can't go to school like this," I said. Dad promptly picked up the telephone and called a lady from church who was a beautician. She quickly arrived and styled my hair into the smooth ponytails I was used to. Dad explained that the only thing he was used to braiding was a horse's tail on the farm.

When I was older, I sometimes typed Dad's sermons on Saturday nights. Then on Sunday mornings, I sat silently in my seat, mouthing the words to myself, helping him deliver his sermons.

When I was studying in Spain and reeling from calls of "Negrita, Negrita"—a name ascribed to black women deemed exotic—by local Spanish men, I was feeling insecure about my blackness, about the oddity of being black in a mostly white country. I had expressed my anger and dismay to my parents.

Then one day, I went to my mailbox. There was a letter from Dad. In it, he attached Frances Cress Welsing's paper on race and encouraged me, reminded me that I was a beautiful black woman and to stand proudly, firmly in who and whose I am.

On my wedding day, my dad danced with me, an expected act for such a day for the father of the bride, undoubtedly. Except it was the first and only time in my life I had ever seen my father dance.

And even as I sit here tapping the keyboard on my laptop, I am reminded that it's the little things that mean a lot. Like the time he called me when I was pregnant, just to see how I was feeling.

A Block off the Old Chip

It is always a surprise to me when my father calls. I talk to my mother often. If more than three days go by, I will call her, or she will call me. If my father answers the phone when I call home, he automatically assumes I am calling for my mother.

"Mom's not here," he will say. Or after a few pleasantries, he'll say, "I'll get your mother."

My father's phone calls to me are an infrequent occurrence.

But not long ago, my telephone rang at home. It was my father. My mother was out of town for a few days. I knew he had been suffering from an injury to his back, for which he had surgery years ago, though his pain had become chronic. I also knew he had to be in bad pain for him to call me. I could sense as much in his slow, edgy whisper.

"I don't feel so good," he said. "Can you stop by?"

I did.

In recent years, when I have gone to see him, he is sometimes lying in bed, pain etched across his face. My dad, the strongman, the man I have seen so many rely on over the years for strength and solace, tries to put on a strong face. But I plainly see his pain. If I look deeply enough, I also see the reflection of the young man who spent more than three decades preaching, building communities, and touching lives.

And yet in my photos of him, I am astonished at how young he looked back then, how strong. Now his hair is gray and thinning, and he sometimes forgets things. But some things seem etched in his memory.

Sometimes he still tells the story about how, when I was younger, I once said, "I'm a block off the old chip." It reminds me of how over the years I was so often the example or story in one or another of my dad's sermons. There was the time I threw my bottle out of the car window when I was a baby and my father stayed up all night while my mother worked the night shift as a nurse at the hospital and I cried and howled for my bottle. The next morning, when the store opened, he was right there to buy me another. "She can suck a bottle when I'm walking her down the aisle," the story goes.

He told that story in his last sermon, having decided to retire after thirty-six years as pastor, preacher, and protester. And as he gave that last sermon as pastor, as the thunder in his voice filled the sanctuary, like it had so many times before, though he stood now grayer, the lines and strain from the years etched in his brown face, I sat amid the congregation, watching, listening, admiring the man who submitted to the call to be father to more than just his own.

And amid his farewells and exaltations on his last Sunday as pastor, there was also the old familiar story of my being his one and only "real" daughter.

And right there I was reminded that he might not have been at the basketball or football games, or at the opening of *Oklahoma*, but in so many ways my father was always there for me. He was there when I went to bed at night, and when I climbed into my parents' bed whenever some nightmare made the shadows in my room seem like monsters. He was there, sitting at our dining room table most days at dinner time, and he prayed. Even when he was too tired to say anything else, his eyes heavy and some new crisis weighing on his mind, he prayed, "The Lord will provide."

I can still hear him, even now, though I am grown and many years since departed from my parents' home. I can hear my father's scratchy voice, rumbling, filling our house, like it did more times than I can count, singing, humming some reassuring, old-fashioned Gospel hymn.

And I suspect I always will.

MONICA FOUNTAIN—Formerly a reporter for the *Chicago Tribune*, she covered a variety of breaking news and feature stories, ranging from urban issues to the plight of black farmers. As a freelance writer, her work has been published in national publications, including the *Washington Post,* the *Chicago Tribune,* the *Chicago Sun-Times, Black MBA Magazine,* and *Black Enterprise.* Fountain earned a degree in journalism from the University of Illinois at Urbana-Champaign, and as a British Marshall Scholar she attended the University of Sussex in England, where she earned a degree in politics and economics.

A Presence in His Absence

Lolly Bowean

I think I was about five years old the last time I saw my father. He was a giant of a man, tall, chocolate, dark brown skin with big hands, and a broad smile. His nose softened his face and the sides curved outward, just like mine. His eyes looked like bits of glass shining from his face.

Looking at him was like looking into a mirror. Yet he wasn't at all familiar.

As I stood stiffly, unmoving, my grandmother nudged me toward him, saying, "Girl, that's your daddy." But even then, he was an awkward stranger to me and also to my twin brother.

When he talked to me, I didn't speak back. I just stood there silently, fidgeting my hands, trying to figure out what to do. As he spoke to me, he used big words I didn't understand. That made me feel stupid.

I never forgot that moment.

In fact, from that point on, a slight nervousness gripped my body whenever I found myself surrounded by a large crowd. I'd slowly navigate between bodies, awkwardly staring deeply into the round brown faces of older black men, looking for that same resemblance I saw that day.

Whenever I was at a major sporting event, or protest, or concert, or even in the mall or grocery store, I couldn't help but look for that reflection of myself. I'd wonder, *"Will today be the day that I see my father?"*

I'm not sure exactly when or how my mother and father came to be enemies. And I don't know why he chose to permanently exit my life and never be around.

From what I've been told, my parents had a very troubled relationship. They went their separate ways before I could form any lasting memories.

He never tried to come back.

I never told my mother about that brief visit when I was five, coordinated by my grandmother. And sensing it was a sensitive topic, I never asked her questions about my father and rarely even mentioned him.

Still, there hasn't been a time in my life when I didn't know that he was supposed to play an involved and intricate part in helping me grow up. And though I never knew him, never got to call his name aloud to him, I missed him.

And everywhere I went I looked for him.

By age nine, I began preparing for the day I would see him again.

Since we didn't know each other, I neatly wrote a list of all my favorite things to help him learn about me. I had to rewrite it four times so there wouldn't be any mistakes. I attached my photo, so he'd know what I looked like and I was sure to tell him that my favorite color was blue.

At first I kept the list in a folder, tucked away in my dark blue book bag. I figured I'd offer it up to him, that day we ran into each other. Then I hung it on my bedroom wall, so it would be handy and available for that moment when I'd need it.

After a few weeks I surmised that he probably didn't care about that list. And then, each time I looked at it, I felt as if it were mocking me, reminding me that there was no daddy there to give it to. Eventually, I ripped it from the wall and threw it in the trash.

But even as the weeks, and then the months and years passed, I didn't give up on the notion of seeing my father again.

Through the years there were always constant reminders of my father's absence. At graduation ceremonies, teachers and professors would ask me where he was. Close friends and boyfriends would ask why I never spoke about him. I never had an answer, and let the questions linger with silence. Even when flipping through family photos, only the maternal half of my life was represented. There seemed no shred of evidence of my connection to the man who was my father.

As an adult, when I obtained my birth certificate, there was a blank space where his name should have been.

Eventually, I began scripting in my head just what I was going to say to my father when I saw him again. And over time, that speech would change, even as my emotions and my life did, and he remained the invisible man.

Whenever I accomplished something, I'd adjust the speech. As time passed, it was nice to keep adding to my list of achievements. Each time, I'd comfort myself by saying it was my father who was missing out. Whenever I faced a challenge or hardship, I'd think about my father and muster the courage to keep reaching. I didn't want to be a failure, as I thought him to be.

And even as the text of my speech kept changing, so did the tone. Sometimes it was friendly and kind. At other times, I'd set my heart on greeting him disrespectfully the moment I laid eyes on him, then cutting him down with slurs and profanity. But no matter what, I'd set my heart on telling him all that I'd done without his help.

I could tell him how I had finished high school at the top of my class and that I had graduated with honors from a prestigious university. I'd tell him about my fellowship to graduate school and about the internships at newspapers around the country. I'd talk of my television appearances and all the political leaders and icons I'd met and interviewed. I'd brag to him that I managed to buy a home all by myself, work for a major news organization, run a business, and travel out of the country without one conversation with my father. I'd make him regret having missed out on so much. For all of the hurt he had caused me, I would have my revenge.

Then two days before Thanksgiving in 2006, I got the news. The telephone call came at work. It was a man's voice on the other end, polite but direct. He was calling from North Carolina. The state's Board of Funerals. My father had been found dead on the floor of his house. He had gotten high on crack cocaine, the caller said, and neglected his diabetes. His blood sugar level shot so high he couldn't be saved. He was all alone.

I listened in disbelief as the official told me for the first time my father's full name: Walter Ronald Patterson, and the only few details I know about him: That he was an army veteran. That he played golf and had worked for some time at a small plant. Besides me and my twin brother, he never had any other children and never married.

As the official from the board spoke, all I could think about was my speech that I had revised again and again all those years for the moment I finally came face-to-face again with my father. Mostly, I thought about how I'd never get to recite it to the person it was meant for.

That day, hidden in my car, I wept aloud for the father I barely knew, for the father I had longed for my whole life, for the father I would never get to know or confront.

But it was then, amid my tears, that I realized that even in his absence, in some strange way, my father had always had a presence in my life. His absence gave me ambition. His absence made me want to achieve, in spite of neglect. I realized that rather than destroying me, the absence of one man helped make me a stronger woman.

And perhaps that was the best gift my father could ever have given.

LOLLY BOWEAN—An award-winning journalist, she is currently a reporter for the *Chicago Tribune*, where she writes about minority affairs and covers Chicago's south suburbs. Throughout high school, Bowean worked as a reporter at the *Knoxville News-Sentinel*. She later interned at the *Boston Globe*, *USA Today*, and the *Wall Street Journal* and had stories published in the *Washington Post* while producing work for National Public Radio. She worked as a reporter at the *Times-Picayune* and began working for the *Chicago Tribune* in 2004. At the *Tribune*, she distinguished herself by covering the aftermath of Hurricanes Katrina and Rita in New Orleans.

Flawed, Fallible, but Still My Hero

By R. Darryl Thomas

The earliest photo I have of my dad and me is one that includes my parents and my oldest sister. I'm pretty certain that it was taken in the late 1950s, inside our sixth-floor Chicago Housing Authority high-rise apartment, near Taylor Street and Roosevelt Road in Chicago. Mom kept an immaculate home. In the photo, Dad is holding my big sis, Cheryl, the firstborn, and Mom is holding their second child and first son, me.

I must be about one year old, and that would make Cheryl three. My now deceased sister Cheryl was the first of what would ultimately be three sisters and three brothers—a black Brady Bunch. I am the oldest surviving child, the one with the longest running memory, the one with a perspective on the way things were and what they became, on why my father, ever fallible, is forever my hero.

Dad was a soldier during the early years with his young bride when Cheryl was born. He enlisted, fortunate for him and us, right between the Korean War and the Vietnam escalation and therefore missed any foreign action in which the worst might have happened. While in the army, he became a paratrooper and military sharpshooter (he taught me to shoot and *not miss*). His military training was an attempt to become a member of the elite Special Forces soldiers that would many years later become known as the Army Rangers, though it was for Dad a dream unrealized. Our home with Mom and Dad in Chicago was peaceful, if not blissful, filled with the aromas of Mom's memorably mouthwatering pound cake.

But sometime between the births of another sister and brother, when I was in second grade, the atmosphere shifted dramatically at home, which seemed in hindsight a microcosm of society in general. It was the turbulent upheaval of the early 1960s, and the upheaval in my formerly peaceful home spiraled into a season of violent and traumatizing verbal and physical domestic violence and abuse. In fact, my parents began to have vicious, raging fights and arguments that sometimes escalated to monstrous altercations that horrified my sisters, brothers, and me. Whether or not my brothers and sisters were too young to have remembered, or whether it is the case that they choose not to acknowledge it, those events and that roughly five-year period has profound spiritual, emotional, and psychological impact on us, even to this day.

And while there is never an excuse for domestic violence, I have over the years reflected on those days, searching for understanding, searching for solace. And this much I have come to believe:

As I see it, Dad was raised in an era when it was widely, socially, and conventionally accepted that men were the presumed "heads" of their homes, wielding the rule, enforceable through corporal punishment administered by the husband/father/male figure. Some men of his era felt (obviously *erroneously*) that all of those under their roofs, including their wives, were subject to their corporal enforcement. That Mom had grown up in a home in an atmosphere of domestic abuse and hostility made for a volatile mix in our own.

Theirs was like a scene from Alice Walker's *The Color Purple*. Our home had become a domestic battle zone. Dad hit Mom with his hands and belt. Mom struck back with bats, butcher knives, or whatever resourceful weapons she could create. Chaotic yelling and name-calling filled our house like the sound of thunder on a stormy night. There were the police officers who would show up at our door, at least one jail trip for my father, and always the sheer terror for us kids, for whom life was

like walking on thin ice. It is indelibly etched into my psyche and I remember it as if it happened only ten minutes ago.

I have reasoned that after five years of my parents' insanity, the in-
tervention of family, church, law enforcement, and others—or maybe it
was the epiphany that his marriage, children, and home were at jeop-
ardy—my dad came to himself. And as suddenly as my parents' season
of fighting seemed to engulf our house, it stopped.

They naturally continued to have arguments and disagreements, but
somehow they learned to fight in a far more civilized manner, and my
sisters, brothers, and I all thanked God.

For I believe my folks' domestic violence helped cause my own ten-
dency early as an adult to an unhealthy avoidance of and aversion to
any conflict—something that greatly impacted my marriage and that
may have contributed to its demise. Only after my divorce did I learn
of positive constructive conflict alternatives and that healthy relationships positively, constructively, and squarely confront issues while re-
specting and honoring each individual's personhood.

Dad got it right a lot of the time. I dare say he got it right more often
than not. And even when wrong, his heart was usually in the right place.
He was a great man with a good heart who tried hard and worked
harder, and he was and is my hero.

During the season of our lives together, my beloved, esteemed, and
revered father went far beyond messing up or screwing up. But fortu-
nately, he somehow figured that out, even if his faults and flaws were not
without impact on my own life. For while there is no excuse, I suspect
that my dad's chaos and insanity begat my own chaos and insanity.

Papa Don't Take No Mess

As a boy, somewhere between sixth and eighth grades, I apparently lost
my "natural, righteous mind." As the old folks say in the South, I was
"smellin' myself." I had begun to hang out with my little thug friends.
And even though I was an advanced student with great grades, I began
to ditch school, cutting class in the eighth grade under the influence of

my unsavory friends. But thankfully, in hindsight, in the words of James Brown, "Papa Don't Take *No-o-o-o* Mess!"

In fact, my father maintained a close working relationship with my teachers throughout my formative school years. He chaperoned field trips, visited school events, and was otherwise involved and engaged in my schooling and social activities. There were "classroom moms." But he was the sole "classroom dad." (Years later, I would likewise be a "classroom dad.") Dad was well known and respected at our church, in the community, and at my school. And his back-channel reconnaissance network vis-à-vis my teachers, unbeknownst to his foolish son, was keeping him meticulously informed and abreast of my every move.

The first time Dad busted me and my friends ditching, he said he would let me slide that one time. His rationale was that boys would be boys. But he gave me stern warning that it was my first and last adventure and that there would be righteous retribution if ever I did it again. I was fully aware that Dad was not one to spare the rod. Yet I did it again. And while Dad did not "whoop" his children often, on those few occasions when actually warranted, he was "old school."

Upon discovering my second case of playing hooky from school, the first thing Dad did that evening was to personally escort me to the homes of all twelve or so of my little so-called thug friends. He stood there next to me at each door as I knocked or rang the bell and waited for the adult to appear. Then Dad would do the proper introduction: "Mr. Davis, my son has something to tell you."

He made me tell Ricky Davis's dad that Ricky, our friends, and I had ditched school that day. Dad likewise escorted me to Mrs. Morgan's, Mrs. Evans's, Mr. Hopkins's, Mrs. Lowden's, Mrs. McGowan's, and every one of my other friends' doors. And each time, Dad stood there to ensure that I ratted out each of my friends to their parents. I later learned that their parents administered various levels of punishment and restrictions. In one evening, Dad had successfully broken up our little gang. And afterward, no other thugs ever approached me again because the boys in the neighborhood knew that my papa, Mr. Thomas, didn't take no mess.

Later that evening, my papa kept his promise with a brief and thoroughly effective trip with me to our basement for some good old-fashioned discipline. Without going into graphic detail, suffice it to say, I never missed another day of grade school. I also had perfect attendance throughout high school. The same goes for college, med school, *and* grad school.

Epilogue

Dad's been in heaven for nearly twenty years. My parents stayed married for more than thirty. Dad, at age fifty-two, and by then a minister of the Gospel, an upstanding member of his community, and more important, a good husband and a wonderful father—having imparted a lifetime of invaluable lessons—died of colon cancer.

And yet, rarely a day goes by when he is not on my mind, flawed, fallible, and forever my hero.

R. DARRYL THOMAS—A multidimensional baritone, pianist, choir director, and Hammond organist based in Chicago, he is a protégé of C. Charles Clency, Ph.D., accompanist to Mahalia Jackson. Thomas's accomplishments include performing Mozart's *Vesperae solennes de Dominica* (K. 321) with a 220-voice chorus accompanied by the New England Symphonic Ensemble at Carnegie Hall. Also an information technology specialist, Thomas is an ordained minister and the son of a Pentecostal preacher.

Tupac Is Alive:
A Father's Angst for a Son

John W. Fountain

Virginia—1996

They say Tupac is dead. I saw him just the other morning, or at least his image, sleeping underneath a quilted blanket in a bedroom at my home in suburban Virginia. My sixteen-year-old son, a handsome slender black boy with thug dreams lurking somewhere in his heart, lay quiet and still, peaceful, unaware of my presence. On a desk nearby lay a greeting card with a handwritten message. I wonder if it has come too late.

In one sense, Tupac Shakur is dead, several assassin's bullets tearing away flesh and skull of the twenty-five-year-old superstar gangster rap artist, giving way to coldness and death. In another, he is still alive, even though he has been reduced to an urn of ashes.

Tupac still lives in the hearts of young black boys like my son. They still hear his music extolling "thug life." Still long to be high-rollin' "gangstas" with fast money, fast women, and fast cars. Still crave the gangster life they see in the slick rap-music videos.

This haunting influence entices both ghetto black boys and suburban black boys, Asian, Hispanic, and some rich white boys, although most often the corpse in the body bag is a dead black boy. I've often had visions of it being my son. Of him being scared straight one dark night with a cold gun pressed to his head and someone else's son with a finger on the trigger, except I always imagined it would be too late.

No matter how bad it hurts or how difficult it is to admit, I cannot deny that there's a part of my son that longs to be a thug. At times, he has seemed infatuated with thugdom, gangbangin', and street life, even mystified. He loved Tupac, even had a big poster of the lyrical young star hanging in his bedroom at his mother's. That he would join a street gang seemed only inevitable. It still didn't make it any easier when I learned through relatives that he was in a gang, or any easier to understand.

He spent his younger years in a midsized Illinois university town, surrounded by "good kids" with "good parents" with "good intentions" for their children. He was a typical boy who loved sports, chocolate chip cookies, and cartoons. On some cold winter days when he got home from school, I'd have a cup of hot chocolate waiting for him when he ran through the door. He was a playful, happy-go-lucky kid, who even as a baby was full of energy. Too young to crawl, he would flap his arms and legs, smiling with his deep dimples showing, whenever I played with him. He was so innocent.

We used to make a point of keeping our children away from the bad element of our families. Mainly that meant my wife's nephews, who have long had a penchant for the streets. After we divorced, she seemed less inclined to follow her old wisdom. Mixed signals.

For several years, he lived with me in a Chicago suburb, for a year in a small countryside town in England, for a while here in Virginia. I always took great pains to shelter him from any gangs or even a white school system that too often mishandles young black boys and hopelessly mislabels them before shipping them down the pipeline of alternative schools, illiteracy, and overall miseducation.

Even spending every other weekend around his cousins proved to be too much of an influence on my son. When he went back to Illinois last year to live with his mother, he soon joined their gang.

My efforts seem so inconsequential, or so I used to think. I know now that for as much as I was trying to save my son, there was an equally intense force trying to destroy him. Not the conspiracy that some might think, the kind in which every white face represents the enemy and seeks the oppression or genocide of the entire black race. Of the many funerals of murdered black children I've attended, none of the killers were white. The enemy is more elusive and seductive. It hypes the life of "New Jack" hustlers and bestows a pair of $100 Nike's and overpriced Starter jackets upon poor ghetto boys in exchange for selling crack. It lures them into thug life, never letting on that to live this brand of life is death.

I have told my son this many times, often hugging him and telling him that I love him. He listened, but I'm not sure he ever heard me. I've wondered what is it that so captivates him about thug life. He cannot, or will not say. Maybe it is the need to belong, the thrill of danger and living on the edge, the need to be different, or the misguided expression of young black men who feel otherwise powerless in a society that still seeks to castrate them in one sense or another. Maybe he just really wants to be a thug, or maybe he just needs time.

Except time often works against thugs. Tupac could tell him that, if he weren't dead.

My son is back in my home now, a bit worn and jolted by the realities of thug life. As jolted as his mother, who realizes that neither of us wants to bury a son.

He is sleeping soundly in his room as I read the card from his mother on his desk:

"I love you. I just want you to make something out of yourself. Thug life is dead. Live and be happy."

My Daughter, My Treasure

John W. Fountain

In your brown eyes is the hope of a nation,
The history of queens and kings, of Sojourner Truths, Harriet Tubmans
And golden sunbeams.
In your mahogany skin
Is the reflection of African beauty American style,
Incomparable Nile.
In your face
I see the sun rise and the moon light,
Universe and stars, twinkling light.
Your feet are rooted
In the wisdom of the years
Sown by ancestor slaves in tears.
And your soul baked golden
By that toil and fears
Sown by slaves for years and years.
You are the embodiment of beauty
Creation of God
The treasure that men seek, the treasure I guard
Until that day when
Another man sees as I—your first love—
The treasure you are.
That treasure you are.
My treasure by far.

Revelation

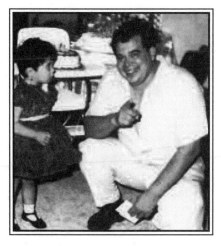

I will declare the decree: the Lord hath said unto me,
Thou art my Son; this day have I begotten thee.
Psalm 2:7

Rosa Maria Santana as a child with her father Cirilo Santana.

A Letter to a Professor:
My Tribute to a Journalism Dad

John W. Fountain

This is a letter I read at a memorial service to my mentor and friend Robert "Bob" Reid, a journalism professor at the University of Illinois at Urbana-Champaign. I wrote it weeks after he passed away and as if I was writing directly to him.

Dear Professor Reid: How are you? I got the Christmas card you sent to me. Thanks very much. I enjoyed our conversation at breakfast, too. It's always a pleasure. You always have a way of making me think long and hard, of challenging me to look inside myself, to look in the mirror, to dig deep, to really embrace compassion and truth.

Truth is, I have known for weeks now that I was speaking here today, and I have only this morning been able to put pen to paper, so to speak. Actually I am in my office, your old office in the "garden level" of Gregory Hall, where we shared far more conversations than I can recall when I was a student nearly twenty years ago. (Has it been that long?) I thought about writing at the apartment, but Monica and the kids are here this morning, so rather than risk disturbing them by all my pecking on the keyboard and my sniffling, I have come here (perhaps it is an appropriate place) to write this: one final letter from a grateful former student to a beloved professor and friend.

I know that I have written letters and emails to you over the years from various corners of the journalism world, in times of triumph and trouble, when my faith was tested. I have written over the years to tell you how much I appreciated our conversations, how much I appreciated you. And while I tend to live my life saying my peace to those I love, giving them their roses while they can inhale the sweet splendor of their fragrance, I regret that I have not said all that there is for me to say to you. So here goes: Thank you for being a father to me.

There simply is no other way to describe it. You see, you couldn't have known before I discovered your office at the University of Illinois, how many times I had heard in my life the words, "You're nothing." How many times I had been told to my face, "You'll never amount to anything." How even as a black student at the university I most often felt as if I didn't belong. How as a student I had known the experience of being barked at by a white professor, his voice dripping with condescension and hostility while in the next breath speaking silken words of praise and comfort to a white student; of how much I had sensed the feeling among peers and teachers that I was not good enough to be a world-class journalist someday; of the damage that this can inflict on one's psyche, on one's soul. Over the years, particularly as a black man, I have come to know well the look, the recognizable, penetrable, cold stare that says, "why are you here, how did you get here, you're nothing."

That is why this morning, as I recall memories of you, my eyes have been wet with tears and my heart so filled with love and appreciation for you.

For in your eyes, I never sensed hostility. In your heart, I sensed only passion for students and for this noble calling called journalism. In your words, I always felt nourished and uplifted. In the wisdom you imparted—even when it had less to do with journalism and more with life—I always sensed faith and fervor. And it mattered not that you are white and that I am black, but that we are both human. That is what I always sensed mattered most in your eyes that saw no racial boundary to human decency, mutual respect, or care for your fellow man.

And even when my papers were splattered with blood-red ink from your corrections, I never once questioned your fairness or the steadfastness of your faith in me as a student of journalism, as a human being.

For all students, you were truly a beacon. For those of us, like Ismail Turay, Sabrina Miller and Raven Hill, who happen to be minority students, you were our lifeline. You never offered us coddling, but a challenge to commitment. Not a hand out, but a hand up. You didn't lower the bar, but you raised it, then expectantly waited—all the while cheering, chastising, prodding and praising when we reached it.

They told us to be brief today, Prof. Reid. But I know that wouldn't have stopped you. In fact, you likely would have taken it as an invitation to extend your allotted time by about an hour (*smile*). But I will adhere to the powers that be.

By the way, Ismail is still serving in Iraq. He said in an email from Iraq that he had prayed you would still be around when he returned from his tour of duty and that he was sorry he never got to say what you meant to him. I told him that when we last spoke in October, you said you had no regrets, that teaching—for the love of students, for the love of journalism, was your life's calling. I told him that you knew how your students felt—how we really felt. Still, I know Ismail would want me to tell you that he loves you and that you were "like a father to me."

Well, Prof. Reid, before I sign off, there is one more memory I want to share. We've not talked about this since. But it was for me a defining moment in our relationship as friends. Years ago when I was applying for admission to graduate school here, you pulled me to the side one day and shared something you thought I needed to know, not as much for the present then as for the future. It was a letter that a former editor at a newspaper at which I had interned had written on my behalf for admission. I asked him for a letter of recommendation and he had agreed. But unknown to me, he wrote a letter saying that I should not be admitted. You shared that with me because you thought I needed to know, because you thought there was a lesson in life to be extracted, even from something that did me no good. The candor and care that you showed me in that instance spoke volumes—not as much as a mentor, professor and friend—but about your compassion, your decency as a human being, as a man who believed in me.

So this afternoon, I celebrate you as I will each day forward. With every story I write, I celebrate you. With every book, I celebrate you.

Every time that I mentor a student, with every breath I teach, every single time I stick the key into the lock at 23 Gregory Hall and walk into *our* office, every time I look into my son Malik's and my daughter Imani's eyes and know that their future is much brighter because I knew Robert Reid, I celebrate you.

I cannot say that I will be here teaching for twenty-five years or twenty or ten, or even two. But for as long as I am here, I will endeavor to do it much like you: with passion, with commitment and with the understanding that unless I help somebody as I pass along this way, then my living has been in vain. That in the end it is about the student.

It really is about the student—not writing books that collect dust on shelves or the titles and prizes one can accumulate within or from without the walls of academe. It is not about the glory of acclaimed scholarship, but about the living testaments—the flesh and blood and souls of young men and women who can effect change for many generations to come. Students. It is about students. It has to be about the student.

Thank you, my professor, my mentor, my friend, my father in journalism and so much more.

Until we meet again.

Love,

John

Papí

Rosa Maria Santana

My dad was a mystery to me. When I was a little girl, he was an intriguing and charming mystery. As I grew older, he became a more perplexing, sometimes painful puzzle. The faded picture of the two of us that I have kept for all these years says as much.

In it, I am three, wearing a red ruffled dress, white socks, and black shiny shoes. My dad kneels next to me, pointing at the camera, trying vainly to get me to pose with him. Instead, I stare at him. Years later, I stare into that grainy snapshot while also searching the pages of my mind over a lifetime of memories for answers to the mystery man and to what caused the picture-perfect daddy and daughter to divide.

As a little girl, I called him Papí. I adored him. As I grew older and spoke more English than Spanish, our relationship became more strained, more distant. I stopped calling him Papí. Instead, he became Dad. I became, in one sense, daddy's grown-up little girl, left with more questions than answers.

Back in elementary school, I did my homework in the dining room, where I cherished my bird's-eye view of Papí in the living room. After a long day of work, Papí would lie on his stomach while watching TV. During commercials, he'd turn over on his back and rub his tummy. In those moments sometimes, I'd sneak up on him, then suddenly jump on his big belly as if it were a trampoline. I was only six or seven years old, but he acted like I weighed a thousand pounds. He'd yell in Spanish: *¡Ah! ¿Qué andas haciendo? ¡Ya para!* Translation: What are you doing? Stop it!

Sometimes, his choice words were a bit more colorful, but he was always playful. I'd giggle uncontrollably. His reaction only encouraged me to keep jumping.

When I was a little girl, I remember him laughing a lot, his laugh resounding like the thunderous crash of waves against ragged rocks. That sound could fill a room as easily as the scent of freshly baked chocolate chip cookies. His laughter was just as reassuring as cookies– a favorite comfort food of mine. I remember him smiling, enjoying food, savoring a good joke.

But as I grew older, something happened. Papí changed. He grew more withdrawn, with pronounced mood swings that I did not—could not—understand as a child, or even later as a teenager. This much I did understand: The twinkle in his eye faded. His boisterous laugh disappeared. He disappeared. And we grew apart.

By the time I was a teenager, our relationship had suffered too many missed conversations and opportunities for father-daughter intimacies. It was precious time and moments made irrecoverable by the years that passed by as school and a career in journalism carried me far from home, farther from Papí.

Bad News

My older brother's voice was frantic over the phone. Was I sitting? He wanted to know. I was. I was at work, writing a story on deadline on my first week as a reporter with a newspaper in Texas.

My brother's voice quivered. In the background, someone sobbed uncontrollably.

"What's going on?" I asked.

He blurted it out. No preliminaries: Dad killed himself. *Dad killed himself...*

His news made me numb. I'm sure he told me other details during our conversation that spring in 1996. But I can't remember them. A tidal wave of feelings swirled inside of me—anger, confusion, disbelief, loss, sadness and guilt, lots of guilt.

The day after my brother's call, I was on a flight back home to help plan my father's funeral. I remember sitting alone in a nearly empty plane. I had slept only two or three hours, but I wasn't tired. I couldn't believe that my dad—a complex yet resilient man—had ended his life by his own hand, though I later reasoned that his life must have been as painful for him as his death was for me.

On the plane, I stared without focus out the window. *What was my life going to be like without a father?* I wondered. I was twenty-nine, no longer a girl, a woman now. But in many ways, I still needed him and had always known that no matter the status of our relationship, I could at least always reach him.

I did not cry. As I stood behind the pulpit where I read my eulogy, I looked at his closed gray casket and it hit me: He was gone. He would never meet my future husband. He would never meet my future kids. He'd never see me progress in my career as a journalist. With his suicide, he denied both of us the chance to share these life experiences. I felt rejected. It hurt profoundly.

It was equally hard to come to terms with my guilt. Why wasn't I there for him? Why couldn't I have helped him?

After I gave my eulogy, I cried.

Revelations

Spring remains a rough time for me because it is at springtime that I remember the details: the eulogy I gave at his funeral, the casket slowly sinking into the earth as I said my last good-bye.

The sting of my dad's death isn't as hurtful as it was back then. But I still miss him. I still cry, though in the days after my dad's funeral and in the years that have followed, I began piecing together his state of mind leading up to his death in my own search to uncover the mystery of the man I once called Papí.

His business was suffering. He was irritable. The last time I saw him, a month or so before his death, he and I argued, though I don't re-member specifics of the quarrel. Others told me he was depressed. At that time, I had been living in Chicago, then later in Texas, busy pur-suing my career while he was in so much turmoil.

My dad and other Latinos from his generation weren't encouraged to openly talk about their feelings. Many of these men stoically endured life—did not invest in $100-per-hour therapy sessions, exploring their emotions or sorting their feelings. Dad felt more comfortable speaking in Spanish than English, and he didn't meet many Spanish-speaking therapists. He was a self-employed entrepreneur who ran his own neighborhood grocery store in South Los Angeles. He couldn't afford health insurance, much like many other immigrants.

Dad's pain began many years earlier, back when he was four or five, selling bags of dry roasted peanuts and *raspados*—flavored shaved ice sold in a paper cone—in his *pueblito*'s town square in the Mexican state of Jalisco. His pain took hold when his parents told him, when he was seven or eight, that he had to work in the fields, mastering a hoe.

My dad never went to school. He was never formally educated to read or write. But he had a strong work ethic—and was always in search of work. He migrated north to Tijuana for jobs. He eventually came to Southern California in the 1950s, back when overt racism against Mex-icans was a way of life in Los Angeles.

Dad, who was sixty-two at the time of his suicide, was alone when he died, though I suspect he may have felt that way for many years. I've tried to imagine what those last harrowing hours were like for him. Al-though his suicide ended his pain, it was the beginning of mine.

Life for me callously moved on. I awoke each morning to face each day as best I could, even though the questions and loss of my dad vexed my soul. A month after my dad's funeral, I flew back to my new job in Texas, where at first I kept secret how he had died. I finally told my boss after he noticed my difficulty concentrating. I eventually endured hours of therapy and Survivors of Suicide meetings. I read newspaper stories about suicide to learn about the experiences of others. Still, I felt empty—until one night, now many years ago.

That was the night that, in a dream, Dad visited me. I stood outside his South Los Angeles grocery store, then walked in and found him waiting for me. He hugged me and asked me to forgive him. He was crying and kept asking me over again for my forgiveness because he said he knew he had hurt me.

I told him that I loved him and I hugged him tight. His wavy black hair felt wet as it usually did, the result of my dad having wet his comb before he ran it through his curly hair. I could smell faint traces of his cologne as he hugged me, even in the dream. It was him. Papí.

When I awoke, I felt peace.

That dream became my turning point. It was for me another reminder that my father was not a perfect man. It was also a reminder of the power of forgiveness. In my dream, he had asked me for forgiveness. And if I was willing to forgive him, I reasoned, why shouldn't I also be willing to forgive myself?

In time, my crying stopped. Slowly, I began to laugh again.

Epilogue

To this day, there are memories of him that I hold as dear as our decades-old snapshot. There is one in particular:

When I was six or seven years old, Papí took me on one of his business trips to Tijuana. At the end of the day, we went to a bakery—a *panadería*. As Papí grabbed pieces of sweet bread with tongs, a girl who looked my age ran into the bakery and snatched a piece of bread before turning around and saying something to the baker. The baker yelled back angrily. The little girl was barefoot and wore a dirty dress. She had gum on a toenail. Her black hair was in a messy braid. Her appearance frightened me. I stepped closer to Papí. I thought the girl was brazen, though the whole truth was she had stolen bread because she had no money and was hungry. At the time, I didn't understand that.

Papí immediately insisted on paying for the little girl's bread. His act of kindness that day left a lasting impression on me. The little girl scared me, but Papí defended her and paid for her bread, and in doing so, taught me an important lesson: Treat people who are less fortunate than you with compassion and without judgment.

Papí rarely went to church. I don't remember ever seeing him pray. But that day, he taught me more about God's mercy than the countless Sunday sermons drummed into me over the years. And this much I have also reconciled: My dad's life was made up of remarkable triumphs and heartbreaking failures, a mixture of happiness and deep sorrow. He became a smart and savvy merchant, running his own business and sending two of his three children to universities. Still, in the end, he may have felt his life didn't count for much.

But he was wrong. He lived a powerful, though sometimes tumultuous human life that still inspires me, even if it still sometimes haunts me.

ROSA MARIA SANTANA—An award-winning journalist, she joined the metro staff of the *Plain Dealer* in Cleveland in 1999. Soon after beginning her new job assignment at the newspaper, Santana, who is Mexican American, received two first-place awards from the Texas Associated Press Managing Editors for her series, *The Quinceañera: Transitions of Life,* for work she did at the *Arlington (Texas) Morning News.* Born in the Los Angeles area, she has worked for the *Chicago Tribune* and is formerly a regional director for the National Association of Hispanic Journalists. She has taught journalism and political science at the University of Southern California, Santa Monica College, Cal Poly Pomona University, Mt. San Antonio College and Azusa Pacific University.

A Tribute to a Father Not-So-Tough-as-Nails

Joseph A. Kirby

I've been told I have skinny legs. Chalk it up to genetics. I have my father to thank for my spindly stalks. With the exception of skin color, my legs are just like his: thin, taut, and muscular. But if you look really closely, just beneath my left kneecap, right above the beginning of my shin, there lies a small mark that distinguishes my legs from his. It is a tiny scar for which I also have my father to thank. Today, it serves as a bittersweet reminder of the man I came to know in his later years as the wisest, funniest, kindest of souls.

But the Joseph Richard Kirby I knew growing up was tough as nails. He wasn't physically imposing, but the icy stare, steely demeanor, and short temper that accompanied his wiry, fifty-year-old frame intimidated men nearly twice his size and half his age. "Mistah Kirby"—as he was known to locals—was the type who ended anything anyone was willing to start.

In the 1970s and 1980s, the bulk of my youth, he held one of the most dangerous jobs in the country: Bronx bodega owner. Kirby's Grocery anchored the intersection of 180th Street and Webster Avenue and bookended our neighborhood's day, its green awning greeting the morning sunshine and its heavy metal gates slamming closed to welcome the night. The bodega's clientele—mainly black and Latino (with the occasional white cop or sanitation worker sprinkled in)—depended on my father for their daily staples: bread, soda, beer, eggs, and cigarettes.

Running a bodega in the Bronx made my father the frequent target of robbers. So often, in fact, that my parents stopped counting the times. But petty crooks who roamed the borough often got more than they bargained for from my strong-willed dad, a machine of a man who worked eighty hours a week and never seemed to break down.

On several occasions, my father, who stood under six feet tall and weighed about 185 pounds, foiled robberies with his street smarts and barrel-chested instincts. Once, a teenage gunman tried to rob my father's convenience store. My father would have none of it. He instinctively reached across the counter, grabbed the shotgun, and nearly wrestled it away in a struggle that spanned the countertop, the floor, and then spilled onto the sidewalk outside.

In the end, the robber got away. But he knew never to set foot in my father's store again. So did the bystanders who had looked on as he writhed on the concrete with a youth three times his junior.

"I don't want their money," my father later said about the group that had stood idly by as he fought for his life, noting that someone should have come to his aid. "What I needed was their help."

It was another small, telling lesson in manhood. That's what my dad was about. Some of his teachings were simple: No turning of the cheek twice. No disrespecting your family. No free respect—everyone had to earn it.

Not a Man of Many Words

Perhaps it was his upbringing. My father was stoic in the way Caribbean men tend to be. Maybe it was because he became a father for the fifth time later in life (his second marriage was to my mother). Or maybe he seemed stoic because, like many fathers and sons, we had different interests: He liked country music, I liked rap. He loved the New York Mets. I turned out a Yankees fan.

Whatever the reason, my father wasn't a big talker. The words between us never came easily. Neither did bonding. Instead, he led by example. Concerned that my doting mother and grandmother were fussing over me way too much, he tried to show me how to be as tough as he was.

One Sunday my father had closed the store early, and because his beloved Mets did not have a game, he decided to work on a storage cabinet that he'd grudgingly promised to make for my mother. He was not the most accomplished carpenter, but he fancied himself handy. And I always marveled as he worked with his hands, often sitting on his knee.

That Sunday, materials and tools of all kinds lay scattered across the kitchen floor when I asked my father if I could help, as I often did. He quickly pointed to a spot beside him. And within a split second of my father's agreeing, I had lunged toward his side—knees first. That's when it happened. I fell, knees first, on one of several nails sprawled over the floor. A five-inch mini-dagger ripped through flesh and cartilage, penetrating my knee, burning like a hot knife.

My mother went apoplectic when she saw that the nail had plunged more than halfway into my leg. She screeched. I needed immediate medical attention, she told my father. My father shushed her and told her to calm down. Then he looked me in my tearing eyes, for a few seconds reassuring me with his gaze. "It's going to have to come out," he said to Mom and me.

Then looking me straight in my eyes, and never once turning away, he slowly tugged on the nail, which pulled on the tissue inside my leg. I groaned loudly but refused to cry while my father kept tugging until he had removed it. Through it all, I never shed a tear. My father could not have been prouder. He told me so as we drove to the hospital at my mother's insistence. My knee hurt for days. But its recovery was speeded by the balm that was my dad's admiration.

That moment was never spoken of again.

Surprise, Surprise

Seasons and years carried me past grammar school, past high school and college, away from the Bronx and my father's bodega, to Chicago and the start of a career as a journalist. A promotion carried me back to New York as a national correspondent. By then, my skin had hardened to a shell, just as my father had wanted. Except, in my rush to blaze a career path and make my family proud, I had drifted away, away from family, more specifically away from my father.

During those years when I had been busy building a career, my father and I chatted. But we didn't "talk." And even when we did manage to catch up, we often didn't have much to say to each other. Small talk was not in the genes.

Then one day, about three years ago, I got a phone call, a call that would change my life. That would change our lives. That call confirmed that my father—a horse of a man, who at eighty-five looked fifteen years younger and still worked six days a week—was indeed only mortal. Days after he'd urinated a stream of blood, my father was diagnosed with prostate cancer.

Once again—this time as a man, though no less his son—I rushed to his side. The news was not good. The cancer had spread throughout his body and metastasized in his bones.

My father was going to die.

What bothered me was not that he was going to die as much as the fact that despite having spent a lifetime with him, having spent much of my adult life asking questions of others, I did not know my father as well as I should have, not nearly as much as I wanted to, as much as I needed to.

In the month that followed the news of his cancer, my father stayed home and, with medicine and rest, regained much of the weight he had lost in the months leading up to the diagnosis. Having taken a self-imposed respite from the nine-to-five workforce, I was in the throes of making a return to work. Instead, I decided to raid my 401K and try to spend as much time and as much money as I could to learn about the man who had taught me so much. It was a decision I know now that I will forever cherish.

Over the course of the next eighteen months, I would get to know his Social Security number and prescriptions by heart. But in the process of visiting him at home several times weekly, accompanying him to nearly every doctor's appointment, taking him to Florida to watch his Mets' spring training, and joining him and my mother in Las Vegas for a week of playing the slots—one of his favorite activities—I learned so much more.

I learned that my dad liked to get up early, 5:30 a.m. or so. Always, no matter the weather. He liked light breakfasts—coffee, maybe some buttered bread. He liked to read the *Daily News* (not the *New York Post*). He still lived and died with the Mets. His favorite number was 154, a portion of the license plate from our first family car.

He liked action movies, Westerns, and daytime TV. He loved working, opting to return to his six-day week at an auto body shop where he was a cashier after regaining some weight. Gospel music found its way into his musical repertoire.

He loved good, dependable people. And, surprise, surprise, he loved to laugh.

The more I saw him, the more I came to see that the stern, cold man I had remembered as a child had thawed. I came to appreciate his idiosyncrasies and company, and he mine.

Epilogue

One crisp Sunday afternoon, in the midst of running errands, I got a call on my cell phone. It was my dad.

Was something wrong? I asked.

"No," he said, "I just called to talk." We spoke for about ten minutes—about my girlfriend, about the weather, about family and current events.

When I told him I'd have to call him back, he told me not to worry.

"I just wanted to say 'Hi,'" he said.

We said good-bye.

The next morning my phone rang. It was my mother. Her voice was hoarse. She gasped and tried to speak.

"*Tengo mala noticia.*" (I have bad news.)

She gulped and fought through the tears that were choking her.

"*Papi se murio.*" (Your father died.)

He had died in his sleep after enjoying a night of watching TV with my mother. He passed peacefully, calmly.

I wept for a few minutes, tears of sadness and, strangely, also tears of joy.

I later learned that my father had spent much of that day on the telephone, calling friends and relatives. I was his last call.

Someday, when I have children, I hope to tell them the story of how my father scarred me for life—in a good way.

And as a loving father someday, I hope to do the same for my own children.

JOSEPH A. KIRBY—A writer and editor whose work has been featured in the *Boston Globe, Chicago Tribune, New York Newsday, New York Times, Washington Post*, and *Black Enterprise* magazine, he is a native of the Bronx, New York. He became interested in journalism after a grade-school classmate's shooting death was chronicled in a local tabloid. After graduating from New York University, Kirby joined the *Chicago Tribune*, where he was soon promoted to national correspondent. He currently runs Between The Lines, a corporate communications and writing firm.

An Open Letter to a Father: A Plea to a Wayward Son

John W. Fountain

This is a real letter, written in response to a note from a friend rearing a son on the verge of leaving home and written also to that wavering son drawn too soon to leave home, lured away by the fast life. The names have been changed.

Hey, Jim and Jamal:

How are you? I have not dropped off the face of the earth, though it seems that I have been snowed under for months. ... All of this to say that I have finally figured out that time isn't likely to get any more plenteous over the next few years, particularly as I have all but signed on to write a new book and I am moving in a new direction in my ministry, all with a wife and children to take care of. *(Hey Jamal, you sure you want to grow up, man? Smile)* Anyway I wanted to touch base and to prayerfully, considerately respond to the developments with Jamal.

Jamal, let me say first that what I say to you is meant in love and comes from my concern for young black men, as a black man with three sons of my own. That said, I have to say that I had hoped I would hear from you after the last note that I sent, though I knew when I wrote it that I probably would touch a nerve—that my words might either draw you, so to speak, or drive you. I sensed the "rebellion" in you and the internal fight to overcome your past while being tugged at by those forces.

I was once a young man, too—one who was angry and deeply bitter at one time with the world, angry with my mother and father and even with God. As a teenager, I often wondered why God had allowed me to be born into my situation—poor, black, pressured, mistreated, stressed—even as a little boy—about grown-up problems. I didn't want to hear anyone, didn't want to conform to rules, didn't want to share the hurt I was really feeling inside. I decided instead to cry alone at night, until I finally decided that I wasn't going to cry anymore, just be bitter and act like I didn't care about anything anymore. That kind of bitterness can turn to rage and rage can destroy those around you and ultimately your own life. The devil intends that end for you. But Jesus Christ gives us the power to alter the course of life's circumstances.

That said, your greatest fight, Jamal, in case you haven't figured it out yet, is not from the enemy without, but the enemy within. It is the man in the mirror. It is yourself, your fears, your lusts, your rebellion from the things of God. God ordains order. And His plan for order is illustrated in our lives every day in the simplest things of life that we often take for granted: our families, our workplaces, our government and society. In all of these cases, there is an established leader and established roles for each of us. When you have a family someday, there will be rules of your house that will be in place to establish order and for the protection and well-being of your sons and your wife and all who are in your house. You will be protector, provider and caregiver. And you will do all you can prayerfully and in God's will to keep the peace of your house, to make it a loving safe place for those that God has given you charge over. And as a good man, you will do this, even when it means making tough decisions. I suspect that sometimes you will make those tough decisions with tears in your eyes and wondering if you are doing the right thing. But my prayer is that you will do what is right in the sight of God.

All of what I have just said is true of me. My worst enemy was John Fountain: my bad decisions, my own lusts, my rebellion, my hurt, my bitterness, my pain, my distrust ...

I would have been lost had I not found a friend, though it seemed the unlikeliest of friends—my grandmother. She was years my elder and gray, and "sanctified," and also a woman. I was young and "knew it all," not interested in church and, of course, I was a man. Yes, I was a man, my own man. I would have preferred to have as a mentor my father, or some man who had endeared himself to me, who had decided to become my mentor and friend. I wished my uncle—my mother's brother—had taken *me* to baseball games, like he did some of my other cousins. But he didn't. And my father never showed up. Then he was dead.

But over time, in conversations with my grandmother, I came to trust her, to develop a relationship with her beyond grandson and grandmother—as friends. That was possible because I realized that of all the people in the world, this woman accepted me for who I was and loved me purely just because. Just because. I later learned the term "agape"—which is the love of God, unconditional and all encompassing, without conditions, pure, whole and true.

As a man now, I often reflect on my grandmother's love. And even though she has since gone on to be with the Lord, I still feel her love, even as I am writing to you. Her love is ever with me, ever speaking, ever pulling for me, ever smiling and saying, "I believe in you, John Wesley Fountain." She called me a "great man" when I was yet a boy. She used to get excited when I signed my name "attorney at law." Her eyes danced whenever I had won some new award in school. When I cried, she cried. When I testified in church, sometimes barely able to speak, she stood across the way, lifting her hands to the Lord and exhorting me to hold onto God's unchanging hand. She spoke life into me, and eventually her love helped begin the mending of hurts of childhood. Of all the people who have ever and who will ever love me in this world, my grandmother's love will always be most special because of the love I saw in her eyes for me, a love that made me feel whole.

So what does this all mean? What am I trying to say?

One of the hard lessons I learned in life, Jamal, is that we have to accept who God sends us. Sometimes what we need does not come from those who ought to give it, or from those from whom we might expect it. Sometimes it comes from unsuspecting, unlikely people, who have said "yes" to the Lord and who are willing to allow God to make a difference in someone else's life through their own. It is no accident that Jim found you, or that you found him, or that God brought you into each others' lives. And it is not happenstance that Jim and his family brought you into their home and have prayed for you and loved you as their own son. It is the love of God and their compassion and concern for you that have led them to speak life into your life. It is their concern and love for you, even now, that keeps them awake some nights worried about you and seeking the counsel of friends and family.

I remember being seventeen and being in a hurry to get out on my own; I remember thinking that the adults in my life were "squares" and always hatin' on me; I remember thinking that I knew better for my life than anybody. I remember the fears that I never shared with anyone and the times when I wondered how everything was going to work out in my life, the times when I wished I had someone I could confide in and trust. I also remember my own defiance, how I wanted to do it my way, no matter what anyone else thought or had to say about it. That was twenty-eight years ago, and I am now forty-five. It is scary to look back now and realize how much I didn't know then and how, if it were not for the grace of God, I would be dead and buried or in prison, or cracked out of my mind, like so many of my childhood friends.

Jamal, I can imagine that in your short lifetime already you have seen more than you should have seen, that you have experienced more than you should have, and that even as you look back at how far you've come from your home, you likely feel as I do—that someone must have been praying for you. As you go forward into this new chapter in your life, I have to tell you that I wish it had not come to this so soon—to the point where it may be either do or die—to a place in life we often call the crossroads.

The support and shelter—naturally, spiritually and socially—that Jim and his family have provided is the kind of structure that my grandparents provided for me. And I think that you are not ready for what is out there in the world should you decide that you can no longer abide by their rules and that the time has come for you to make a go of it on your own. The world can be a cruel place, as you well know. And it is especially cruel to black men who are not equipped with the education and economics (money or ability to take care of yourself) that we all need to survive. That said, *you* can make it! But I think you will find the same rules that were apparent in Jim's house and in the homes of most functional families, to be the same rules that are needed for success in life:

Be Accountable (Let folks know where you are and what you are doing.)

Be Honest (Tell the truth to your family, to your employer, to everyone with whom you interact and to yourself.)

Be on Time (In fact, be early.)

Work Hard (Nobody likes a sluggard.)

Maintain Self-Control (That means your anger and your passions. Just because it looks good, tastes good or feels good doesn't mean it is good.)

Use Clean Language (Your speech betrays you. In other words, what comes out of your mouth speaks volumes of who you are.)

Keep Good Company (The Bible says that evil communications corrupt good manners. If you want to soar with eagles, don't hang out with buzzards.)

Seek to Improve Yourself (Nobody owes you anything. We must seek as men to equip ourselves with the knowledge and resources that will lead us to a world of possibility.)

Don't Blame Others for Your Mistakes (Confess and acknowledge your faults and seek forgiveness, and choose to live differently.)

Don't Just Dream (Be a doer: work, plan, build and dream.)

Don't Burn Bridges (Don't mistreat people who have opened their hearts and their doors to you; don't speak harshly to them; don't falsely accuse them; don't allow your own bitterness and anger to spill out at them so that you cause them pain and sorrow, so much that if you ever needed to go back to them [to cross that bridge again] they would be unwilling to allow you to do so. In other words, you will have burned that bridge to the ground.)

Trust in the Lord "with all thine heart and lean not to thine own understanding. In all thy ways acknowledge Him and He shall direct thy paths." Proverbs 3:5–6

Okay, I know I write long, and I am coming to an end. But I am praying as I write that I am led of Him and that something I have said blesses you both (Jamal and Jim), if only in some small way. Let me begin to conclude by sharing a story:

I know a young man whose father loved him dearly, and who embraced his son, who tried in every way to let his son know how much he loved him, even though the father and mother had divorced. As much as the father showed his love, whether it was by gifts or simply by his presence in his son's life, the son seemed enchanted by the elements of ghetto life, particularly thug life. The mother's relatives were involved in gangs and criminal activity, and it wasn't long before the son began to see his father's lifestyle—lawful and disciplined—and his expectations for his son while he was in his house, as being the less desired life of the two. Maybe it was that the father's way of life was not so much less desirable than thug life as it was that his father's way was structured, disciplined, requiring his son to work hard at school, to do chores, to be in by a certain time, to always let him know where he was going, to be truthful and honest—always—to be respectful, to go to church on Sundays, to eat meals *with* the family sitting around the table at supper time, to read more than playing video games, to not wear some crazy haircut with some design carved into his head, to follow the rules of the house and to set an example for those behind him.

To make a long story short, the son was living with his father, who had taken him back into his home after the son had abandoned the father, hiding out one summer with his mother while visiting her in Chicago, basically because he didn't want to abide by the rules of his father's house. Upon his return to his father's house a year later—and after having lived without rules, ripping and running the streets (as the old folks used to say) with his homeys—the young man seemed to be going along with the rules, though he was under constant watch. In that time, the father and his house seemed to be coming unsettled by the tension of it all. Mostly, it was the son's rebellion, though it wasn't in what he said or did, but in his quiet resistance—the lies, the sneaking around, the son's attempt to see how far he could bend the rules without actually breaking them. Then one day it became clear, as clear as the morning sun, as the father sat one day after one more lie and act of rebellion, that in all this time, the son had not changed on the inside and instead had simply been going through the motions. His heart and perspective had not changed. My son had not changed.

Yes, he was my own son. And he was going on nineteen when I decided that it was best that he leave. Every decision I had made regarding him up to that point was with his best interest at heart. But it was—*he* was—tearing us all apart. And for the sake of my family, for the sake of my own sanity, I knew what I had to do, even though I did not want to do it.

We were living in Virginia then. I called that evening and made a plane reservation for him and asked him to pack his bag. My wife and I drove him hurriedly to the airport that night and I walked hurriedly through the gate and hurriedly led him to his flight and said good-bye, then hurriedly left the airport. I hurried because if I did not I'm afraid I wouldn't have been able to put him on that plane. I know I would have broken down and cried. Instead I cried on the way home and for many days after. But years later, I still know it was the right decision and that it ultimately was a decision that my son had made—not me.

Jim, I sense in your words a love for Jamal that he cannot comprehend right now. I sense in your concern and your reaching out for answers—in no doubt, your cry to God for counsel and direction—that you love this young man like your own son. And to say that I admire that in you would not suffice to describe the way in which that moves me. I see in your act and commitment of love, the love of Jesus Christ. And while I know it is painful—speaking as one father to another—to see a son, ill-equipped, decide to go out into the world, know that the one who led you to Jamal and who led Jamal to you is able to keep him and to redeem him. So I exhort you to keep praying, keep believing, keep trusting God to work on Jamal's behalf. Keep asking God to keep him from the enemy, to put good people in his life, to protect him in his own folly and to heal him and lead him into the path of the purpose for which He has ordained him from his mother's womb. It hurts, I know. My heart still hurts and I am fighting tears, even as I am writing and remembering my son. But he and I are in God's hands, and His grace is still sufficient.

My prayers are with you both. God bless you both. Please keep us in your prayers. You are in ours. Peace.

Your brother,

John

Finally, Peace for a Son

John W. Fountain

There was a rap at the front door of our apartment on the West Side of Chicago that evening. Mama and Net and I sat on the sofa, watching television on a quiet night at home. It was dark outside. The sound of the flickering television filled the living room. Back then, Mama loved watching "*The F.B.I.* in color, with Efrem Zimbalist, Jr.," as the announcer's voice blared over the television at the start of every episode and we sat sometimes with a bowl of buttered popcorn. She also liked watching *Bonanza* and *The Rifleman*. We liked watching whatever Mama watched, especially at night over popcorn, sitting at Mama's feet in our pajamas under the glare of the television.

The knock on the door that evening caught us by surprise. Usually the arrival of visitors at our front door was announced by footsteps on the unpadded wooden stairs that led to our third-floor apartment. There were no footsteps this time. Yet the knock seemed recognizable. I jumped to my feet and dashed to the door.

"It's Daddy, it's Daddy!" I exclaimed.

"Come back here, John," Mama scolded. "Don't open that door."

"But it's Daddy," I answered, puzzled by Mama's tone of voice.

"How do you know who it is? Wait a minute, don't open that door, ask who it is," Mama fired back.

"Whooo izzzz it?" I asked, barely able to keep still.

"It's me," the voice behind the locked door answered. "It's me, John."

"It's Daddy, it's Daddy!" I screamed, jumping up and down. "I told you it was Daddy!"

Mama responded less excitedly.

"Okay, open the door," she said.

I twisted the lock. There he was. Tall, slender, smiling and wearing a mustache and cap, the patch of pink in the middle of his lips.

"Dad-deee!"

I grabbed his leg and hugged him. He hugged me back, nearly tripping as he walked through the door. He was chewing gum as usual. He smiled.

"Hey boy," he said.

I held onto him all the way to the living room. He spoke to Mama and Net. Then he sat down in a chair in front of the television. He and Mama didn't have much to say to one another. In fact, there was a strange look of unfriendliness or distance or something else in Mama's eyes. Mama seemed nervous. After a few minutes, she arose from the couch and disappeared inside her bedroom, which sat just off the living room. Whatever was their problem didn't matter to me. Daddy was home. I climbed up on his lap. The cinnamon on his breath smelled strong, although there was another strong scent on his breath. It was as if the two scents were wrestling against one another, each trying to prevail. Years later I would recognize the smell that had been on my daddy's breath that night as that of a man who had been drinking and had popped a piece of chewing gum into his mouth to try to camouflage the stale, lingering smell of gin, whiskey, and wine. Sitting there on Daddy's lap though, I honed in on the sweet aroma of cinnamon.

"Daddy, gimmee some gum," I begged. "Can I have some gum?"

Daddy reached into his shirt pocket and handed me a slice of Dentyne. I peeled back the paper and shoved the gum into my mouth. I felt so secure sitting there, resting on his lap, as if nothing else in the world even mattered. I cannot remember the last time I had seen him before then. It was true that by the time I was four, he had already become an irregular in our lives, but there were still fresh memories of being together with my daddy, of his big hand swallowing mine as we walked to my aunt Marguerite's house. Aunt Marguerite was his mother's sister and she lived in K-Town, but down off Cermak Road, about a dozen blocks or so from our apartment on Komensky. A tall brown-skinned woman who didn't mince words, she had three sons, all older than me. Their names were Clyde, Frank, and Peter. And they were already teenagers, with a knack for squeezing my head in their palms and play-fully mocking me with a version of the nickname that Aunt Marguerite had affectionately given me, "fur ball."

"Hey, fuzz ball," my cousins would say, laughing and almost falling over themselves as they spiked my head with their fingers to my own soreness. They thought this was fun and they amused themselves at my expense, although I could sense that this was never done maliciously and I loved being around these guys. They were like goofy big brothers.

I had gone to their house with Daddy many times and had even spent the night there. Many years later, I can still see my father's image as he lay sleeping in one of Aunt Marguerite's bedrooms. Daddy slob-bered when he slept, something that Aunt Marguerite's boys also teased me about. That hurt some. He was, after all, my daddy. I loved that man as much as any little boy is capable of loving his father. It was innate, I guess. It is hard to describe the sense of ease and comfort I felt in his presence, or the reaffirming power and purpose I felt even as a small child just being around him, as if I was his and he was mine. In all of my years, I have never known that feeling again. Never felt completely whole. That is what I felt sitting there on my daddy's lap, chewing cin-namon gum, resting on his chest and pressed close to his face, feeling his mustache and breath and life. I felt whole, like some man's son. I could have sat there forever.

"Hey John," Mama interrupted, "Come here." She emerged from her bedroom with a note. "Take this note downstairs to Aunt Scope," she said matter-of-factly, referring to her sister who lived downstairs.

"I know what this is," I exclaimed, grabbing the folded piece of paper. "You want to borrow some money." That was usually the purpose of my mother's notes to my aunt. I knew as much because I had managed to read them all. Mama did not know this of course. But that was one of the perks of being a smart kid, and knowing how to read. I even used to decode the words Mama and other adults spelled around me without hinting that I knew what they were talking about.

"Boy, just take the note to Aunt Scope like I said," Mama said.

"Gwen, if you need money, I got some money," Daddy interrupted.

Mama didn't answer. Her eyes looked almost afraid.

"John, take the note to Aunt Scope," she said.

I hurried to the door, anxious to get back to my daddy. As I walked down the stairs, I thought about reading the note. I even began to unfold it, but decided not to. I don't know why I chose not to read this note. I just didn't read it. I knocked on the door. Aunt Scope answered.

"Aunt Scope, my mama told me to give you this note," I said handing over the correspondence.

Aunt Scope unfolded the piece of paper and read it.

"Tell her I said okay," she said, half-smiling.

I ran back upstairs in my stocking feet.

"Ma," I said, "Aunt Scope said okay."

"Okay," Mama said.

I climbed back onto Daddy's lap. He and Mama were having some discussion. I cannot recall what they were saying. But the tenor of their conversation was strained, Mama's words careful and shaky. We were all sitting there quietly when a few minutes later, suddenly there was another knock at our door. It was a hard rap and unrecognizable. I jumped up and was about to bolt toward the door when Mama stopped me dead in my tracks.

"Johnnnn, sit down!"

I froze. Mama stood up and hurried to the door. I followed behind her.

"Who is it?" she asked.

A man's heavy but gentle voice answered back, "The police."

The police? Why were the police here, I thought. *What's going on? What? Why? What …*

"Gwen you didn't have to call the police," Daddy said, sounding apologetic. "I just wanted to talk, I would have left."

"There is nothing to talk about," Mama fired back, her voice filled with fire. "I just want you out ..."

The two black police officers in their blue uniforms escorted my father away in handcuffs. I watched as they led him out of our apartment and down the stairs, a piece of me going with them. Afterward Mama explained that she was sorry that Net and I had to see our daddy taken away like that, that she had had to call the police on him. He had been drinking. And we didn't want for Daddy to hurt Mommy, did we?

We didn't. Neither could we understand, although one of my earliest childhood memories was of my father and mother scuffling at the top of a flight of stairs that seemed like the top of a steep hill and me standing there frozen, afraid that at any moment Mama might go tumbling down. She did not. At least not in the physical sense. But looking back, I can only imagine that that was how she must have felt sometimes, left to raise two children, her life spiraling out of control. The night that the police took Daddy away was Mama's attempt to regain control. And how difficult, how brave of her to have summoned the police and to have kicked this man—who obviously had too many problems to be any good for her and her children—out of our lives. But I did not understand this back then. I could not have understood it then.

I don't remember if I cried that night. But for years, I would cry whenever I recalled that night. For years, I would sit on our porch on summer evenings, watching the cars go by and dreaming that one day one of those cars would suddenly pull over to the curb and stop and that the man getting out of the car would be my daddy. Over the years, I eventually forgot what Daddy looked like, as any pictures of him disappeared from our apartment and the portrait in my mind became frayed and fuzzy. Faded too were recollections of what he even sounded like, as months turned into years and years turned into what seemed like a lifetime without word from him and with my mother having made the decision that we should not see him and that he should not see us. There was no use in even bringing up his name or even the possibility of seeing him, unless I wanted to encounter Mama's wrath.

In Mama's eyes, Daddy was no good. At least that was the way Mama and the cacophony of other mamas in the hood, who routinely pronounced their baby's daddies to be just as good as dead, had simplified it. As a child, I sometimes couldn't help but believe that this was true. That daddy was no good. But I discovered life to be more complex and have come to see that men in one way or another are the sum of the experiences of their own, sometimes tragic childhood. I eventually found another way to describe my daddy. Not as being "no good." Just filled up with so much bad that he wound up trying to rinse away his yesterdays with whiskey and cheap wines that left him hung over and staggering through too many todays, until finally there were no more tomorrows.

In all of my forgetting over time, one thing I never forgot: That Daddy always chewed cinnamon gum. Sometimes I would buy it at the candy store just to remember him. Every time I inhaled the scent of cinnamon, I thought of him. Every time I chewed a cinnamon toothpick, or when I sucked on cinnamon candy, or when Aunt Mary sprinkled cinnamon on my toast or on an apple, I thought of my daddy. I still do.

As a child, I vowed that someday when I got good and grown, I would seek out John Wesley Fountain, Sr., if only to restore the portrait of him in my mind, if only to find some measure of wholeness for my soul. Someday I would see my daddy again, someday.

A Surrogate

Eddie walked into the living room and sat on the couch. We talked for a few minutes. It was not much of a conversation. Just a meet and greet, small talk between children and an adult who was a complete stranger, smiles and chitchat. I didn't feel one way or another about this man named Eddie. He was just somebody who was going out with my mom. He was dark. He had an Afro and a mustache. He didn't look ugly. He was chewing mint gum. He was a man. It wasn't like he was going to be my dad or anything.

Within a year, they were married. He moved in with us, which I am sure must have been an adjustment for me. But I cannot remember any particulars other than my difficulty in accepting the idea of calling another man "Daddy." Mama helped with the transition. She told Net and me that daddies are men who take care of their children. Mama has always had this saying, "You have to pay the costs to be the boss." Mama essentially told us that there was a new sheriff in town. You didn't argue with Mama about some things.

The first time I called my stepfather "Daddy," I felt sort of queasy. But I soon got used to it as well as the idea of having a man around the house. That he was willing to allow me to call him "Daddy" and to tell other people that I was his son made calling him "Daddy" that much easier. Whenever he went to the store, I walked with him. I studied him as he fixed things around the house with his bag of tools. I stared at him through the bathroom doorway as he wiped shaving cream over the stubble on his face and carefully raked a razor over his cheeks, chin, and neck until they were smooth. I sneaked into his aftershave, played catch with his baseball glove. He cut my hair, taught me how to shine shoes and play checkers, both Chinese and the usual kind.

He lifted me onto his shoulder and carried me to my bed when I fell asleep some nights or when he and Mama had been out and they picked us up from the babysitter. He became my dad. In fact, just hearing his voice, a man's voice, resonating through our house had a stabilizing influence, like an anchor does for a ship. We didn't share many conversations. He wasn't that kind of man. We played and worked and laughed together. And in time, I grew to love him as a son loves a father. This did not fill the void or heal the pain left by my natural father's absence. But it surely helped sustain me at times. And yet, so many days, I longed for my real father.

Dead Ringer

On Monday night, January 29, 1979, at 10:04 p.m., it was requested by the Evergreen Police Department, (Officer Freddie L. Stallworth) to get blood samples from two accident victims; John Wesley Fountain and Russell E. Brown.

The Evergreen Hospital got only one blood sample. It was from Fountain. These blood samples were to check the blood alcohol content of these subjects.

The result from the blood sample taken from John Wesley Fountain
was 0.26 percent.

At 12:15 a.m., John Wesley Fountain was pronounced dead. It was a snow-blown winter's day on campus, the Blizzard of '79 having painted the landscape a frosty white. I had just arrived back at Champaign that winter when the snow began to spill like an endless waterfall from the skies. It was as if I went to bed one night and awoke the next morning to a vast sea of snow that blanketed much of the Midwest. But life on campus went on as usual, even amid the effects of a blizzard, though in considerably slower motion. Students waded through thigh-high snow, making their way to the center of campus for classes.

I was glad to be back at school but felt under considerable pressure, given that I was on academic probation and possibly facing expulsion from the university unless I brought my grades up. I made a pact with myself that there would be no party-hopping this semester, only serious study, and, of course, working to keep a few dollars in my pocket, maybe even enough to eventually get my telephone turned back on. The pressure weighed heavily on me: Being in college and being a father, being on probation, my lack of finances and my worries about my son and his mother, Mama, my sisters, and my brother. In hindsight, I know that the effect of all of this was that I was sinking into a depression. Weary and laden with the weight of the world was how I felt as I lay across my bed in my dorm room early that evening on January 28, after classes.

I was dead-tired when I first lay down fully dressed and with no intention of going to sleep. I awoke sometime after midnight and looked over at the digital clock on my desk. I was shocked to see that I had slept so long. It was a deep, almost eerie sleep that I will never forget. I felt as if I had been drugged. I got undressed and then went back to bed. The next morning I awoke, showered, and dressed, then went to class. Later that day when I was returning from class, I checked my mailbox, located inside the same building as the snack bar, where rows of metal student mailboxes were housed. Inside my mailbox was a handwritten message that read, "John, please call home." I knew that something was wrong. I thought that maybe something had happened to my son or his mother. I rushed a few feet away to a public telephone.

"Hello-o-o," Mama's voice rang finally on the other end.

"You have a collect call from John," the operator said. "Will you accept the charges?"

"Yes," Mama said, her voice bearing a hint of urgency.

"Go ahead, caller ..."

"Hey Ma, I got the message to call. What's wrong?"

"John Fountain is dead," Mama said. Just like that. *John Fountain is dead.*

There was nothing except silence between Mama and me for a few moments. Mama's words were hard to process. *John Fountain is dead? John Fountain is dead. John who? What? What is she talking about?* I wondered.

"Huh?" I responded finally.

Mama continued. "I got word from Alabama that John Fountain was killed in a car accident last night," she explained.

Finally, it hit me. And I understood what she must be saying: That my father was dead. Perhaps it was the impersonal deadpan way in which Mama had first spoken when relaying the news of my father's death that made it hard for me to grasp her words fully. They were without detectable sympathy or emotion.

"What?" I asked, more as a rhetorical question as Mama explained in more detail.

I stood next to the telephone, students passing by, all of life seeming suddenly to pause, stunned as Mama talked. My thoughts floated a million miles away, back in time and space to memories of holding my father's hand, to the smell of cinnamon gum on his breath and the reddish spot at the center of his lips, to memories of me sitting on my porch on Komensky Avenue on summer days, watching the cars pass by and hoping that someday some car would stop suddenly in front of my house and that the smiling man climbing out of the driver's side door would be my father. Mostly, there were blank pages in my mind, empty black spaces and questions, a million questions that I dreamed of erasing someday when I got the chance to sit and talk with the man whose name and seed I carried. I had no illusions about him or any dreamy misconceptions about the kind of relationship the two of us might ever have established. I simply wanted to hear his voice again, to see his face, to touch him, to look into his face to see if I could see any of me. I needed to know that he was not a mirage, to at least restore to my memory the portrait of the man who had long since faded. As I stood there on the telephone, talking to Mama, tears streaming down my face, I began to sob slightly.

My reaction shocked Mama but also stirred her wrath.

"Why are you crying?" she fussed.

"He was my father," I answered.

"He ain't never done a damn thing for you," Mama said, her anger rising.

"It doesn't matter," I answered. "He was my father."

It was hard for Mama to understand, and perhaps even harder for her to express much sympathy, given that my father had essentially deserted her with two children to raise on her own. I could understand Mama's perspective even back then. But I am still convinced that parents often lack the same understanding about their children's feelings for an estranged parent, particularly in cases where one parent has hostile feelings, even justifiably so, for the other parent—feelings that they tend to try to impose upon the child, often unknowingly. That can place children in an emotional vise, held hostage, not free to love, feel, or think as their heart dictates.

"You are so damn stupid," Mama shouted.

Click! I hung up.

Later that day, calmer heads prevailed. Mama said that services for my father were going to be held on Friday and that my stepfather had offered to drive Net and me to Alabama. Still swirling from a mix of emotions, I said I did not want to go.

"I think that would be a mistake, John," Mama said, although I really wasn't listening all that closely to her. "Okay, so he didn't do anything for you; you can do for him the only thing you could do for him as a son. You can go to his funeral. If you don't go, you'll regret it later."

After some thought, I decided to make the trip to Evergreen to see the man whom Grandmother had told me I looked so much like, even walked, talked, and laughed like, even if John Fountain was now dead.

We walked up the stairs of the tiny Evergreen, Alabama, church, filled with soft white light. The faces of the people inside were all a blur and my mind filled with fog. At the front of the church was an open coffin filled with the remains of the man I'd waited all these years to see. With my mother and stepfather following closely behind us, Net and I walked down the church aisle past the faces on both sides, inching closer toward the coffin.

I was filled with an eerie sense of anticipation. In one sense, I dreaded the moment when my eyes would meet my dead maker. In another, I was anxious to affirm the ghost in my memory.

A few more steps, a few more blurry faces, and I was standing above the coffin.

My eyes rushed toward the face, to the sealed eyes that were unfamiliar. They ran from his hair to his forehead and the cold skin caked with makeup that stirred no memories within me. I followed the lines to his lips, the mustachioed cold lips with the reddish spot in the middle that I recognized instantly. In that moment, it was as if I could smell the scent of cinnamon and a veil was lifted, my amnesia suddenly enveloped by living color and memories of my father brought back from the dead to life. But he was dead. And our reintroduction, delayed by years and a lifetime, was reduced to a few-seconds' meeting between a living son and his dead father, and a tearless, silent good-bye.

As we drove toward the interstate, bound for our more than twelve-hour ride back to Illinois, I was filled with more turmoil than peace, sitting in the back seat of my stepfather's green-and-white Buick LeSabre. The accident report Mama got from the local police station, where I had been mistaken by several people as one of my father's relatives because I looked so much like them, at least bore more answers about what happened that night my father was killed. Mama said she got the police report because she intended to hire a lawyer to find out if there was anything that Net and I might eventually gain financially from our father's being killed in the accident. For many years after my father was killed, whenever I heard the Temptations' song "Papa Was a

Rolling Stone," I always thought of my father, particularly as I sang along to the latter part of the hook: "… And when he died / All he left us was alone." If there was anything to be inherited, Mama, in her doggedness and tenacity, would surely find out. Upon leaving Evergreen that day, all we had was a police report. Interspersed in the details of a violent collision, contained in the four-page report written in ink in an officer's squiggly penmanship, I at least found a sketch of the mystery man:

My father was driving a 1973 two-door Chevy station wagon. He was unemployed. "Drinking—yes" is circled. It was not known whether the truck driver had been drinking. Neither was his blood ever tested for alcohol.

On the night of the accident, the weather was clear, dark and dry. It occurred on a four-lane asphalt highway, Highway 31. My father was going about 5 mph in a 55 mph zone as he pulled onto the road from his mother's driveway. The truck, which was transporting produce, was doing about 40 mph and coming over a hill.

The truck struck the station wagon. My father was not wearing a seatbelt. He was ejected from the car. His head struck the asphalt pavement. He was taken by ambulance to Evergreen Hospital. He was pronounced dead at 12:15 a.m. January 29, 1979.

The cause of death was listed simply as: "Car truck crash on Highway 31 South."

The other thing I learned about my father during our visit to Evergreen was that his nickname was "Crack." At least, that was what everybody called him.

"Crack" had an uncomfortable ring in my ear. I wondered silently how my father acquired such a nickname. I imagined that he might have gotten it from falling down drunk and hitting his head time and time and time again. Or maybe it was something else. I could have asked someone for the answer. Truth is, I did not want to know.

As we rolled farther and farther away from Evergreen, down a stretch of lonely highway, I was admiring the hills of red clay dirt, which I had never seen before. Mama asked if I wanted to take some back with me as a keepsake, something to remember my father by—red clay dirt. I said yes. So my stepfather pulled off the highway to the side of the road. Net and I climbed out of the car and scooped up several handfuls in the Alabama sun. Then we resumed our journey home.

I sank into the white leather seat, having a greater sense of where I came from but no real sense of where I was going, and still many tears and years away from finding any resolution about John Wesley Fountain.

Reconciliation

We drove southwest on Interstate 85, headed down the endless highway toward Evergreen in the July sun. It was a long drive from Virginia to Alabama. My wife, Monica, and my youngest son and I were making the drive that summer of 1995 to my father's hometown, where his mother and some of his siblings still lived. My eldest son had pleaded with me to allow him to live with his mother (my first wife) and our daughter. Tearfully, I gave in to his wishes, though clearly understanding that my son's desire to leave my household was instigated by his mother's desire to disrupt my life any way she could. In taking the job at the *Washington Post*, Monica, my youngest son, and I had moved to Virginia, where life was calmer but where simmering questions that had long vexed me began to resurface, begging for answers. There were still unresolved issues, things that I still grappled with, the kinds of things that I would have to come to terms with in the way that every man who overcomes his past must come face-to-face with his demons.

I had called my father's mother, Autherine Jackson, months earlier and reintroduced myself. Actually, it was more like introducing myself for the first time. The only time that we had met previously was that brief encounter sixteen years earlier when I had come to Evergreen for my father's funeral. This time I was driving myself to Evergreen and hoping to find answers about my father and the side of my family that up until then had been perfect strangers to me.

Though I was on a voyage for answers, I am not sure that I knew all the questions. When I had spoken with Mrs. Jackson, she seemed delighted at the thought of me visiting with the family in Evergreen. I also sensed her shock after all those years, to one day pick up the telephone and hear the voice on the other end introduce himself as John Fountain. That was understandable, especially when the only John Fountain who had ever really been a part of her life was the son who now lay dead and buried for many years.

The closer we drew to Evergreen, the more I worried about whether my father's folks would consider me to be family or whether they would simply see me as some mixed-up young man struggling with some childhood anxiety over his father's absence in his life. I also wondered whether I could handle being in Alabama, where I had not been since the funeral in 1979. The closer we got, the more the internal struggle boiled inside and the more old feelings, memories, and past hurts seemed to surface as if my life were flashing before my eyes.

"Babe, I don't know if I can handle this," I said to my wife, five months pregnant and sitting across from me on the passenger's side.

"John, it'll be all right. Your father's mother seemed happy when you called, right?"

"Yeah."

"And when you told her that you wanted to come and visit, what did she say?"

I sighed. "I know, I know, I just don't understand why nobody down here ever called me or came to see me or anything. I mean, it was almost like I didn't exist. I don't want them thinking that I want nothing from 'em," I said, my anger percolating, though mostly at the root of it was hurt. Hurt and pain.

"All I want is a picture of my dad, and to ask my grandmother some questions," I huffed.

"It'll be all right, John," Monica said, rubbing my hand. "It'll be all right."

Driving into Evergreen was like driving through a cloud of smoke into my past. The roads looked strangely familiar in a sense, as did the police station uptown where Mama, my stepfather, Net, and I had gone that January in 1979 to get a copy of the police report from my father's accident. Soon we rounded the corner on Highway 31 South, where my father had been shot like a missile through the windshield of his car when it was hit by the truck. We traveled north a piece until I spotted

JOHN W. FOUNTAIN   143

the narrow driveway where my father's car had rolled just a few feet
onto the highway into harm's way before the awful wreck happened.
Then we drove up the driveway toward the little redbrick, single-story
house where my father had spent his last hours here on earth, stupefy-
ing his mind and soul, and where his mother—my other grandmother—still lived. I knocked on the door and she emerged, a frail, thin
woman with butterscotch skin and big glasses. I hugged her and we
went inside and talked for a while.

Our conversation was filled with questions. There were questions
that rolled slowly and painfully from my lips. Questions about who my
father's father was, about why my father never came to see me, and
about my father and his family's medical history, which in time had become more important for my own longevity and the well-being of my
children and my children's children.

"I don't know why he didn't come and see you," Mrs. Jackson said,
speaking plain and honest. "We all knew about you and your sister. But
you know, Gwen," she said referring to my mother, "that girl could be
so mean."

I was sitting there thinking that she had some nerve saying anything
about my mama. But I allowed her to continue uninterrupted.

"I don't know," she continued. "You know, your daddy had a drinking problem. I just could never get him to leave that stuff alone. He was
okay as long as he didn't drink. But when he drank ..."

I listened to Mrs. Jackson talk for a little while about how my father
was forced to live with her mother because his stepfather did not want
him living there with his siblings and mother. She spoke of some of her
other sons or relatives who had drinking problems, about the relative
who was killed in an automobile accident, about another whose legs
were amputated because of drinking and diabetes, about one sad
tragedy after another. The more she talked, the more the anger and pain
of a lifetime seemed to fall off me as if I were a snake shedding skin.
And I began to wonder what might have happened to me if my troubled
father, so vexed by all of the demons that plagued not only him but also
possessed his family, had been in my life. I knew how my life without
him had turned out. And while less than perfect, I was not an alcoholic.

I had a steady and respectable job. I had managed to go back to college and earn my degrees despite my hardship. I believed in family and loved my children, who would never know the pain of not knowing their father's love or suffer the image of me to be reduced to a foggy memory.

All that time I had thought myself deprived by not having known my natural father. But sitting there in the living room where his mother's only picture of him hung in an oval frame, for the first time in my life I understood that I was better for having not known him. I actually thanked God for not having known the man and for having given me the good sense to latch onto the best that was in the men who were in my life.

I was the sum total of them all.

From my grandfather, I took his love for God and family and his stewardship. From Uncle Gene, I took his humor and oomph for masculinity and manhood. From my stepfather, I took his kindness toward children, his love of the blues and knack for do-it-yourself fix-up jobs. From Mr. Adams, I took his zest for education and the belief that it had the power to change my life, his perseverance and indomitable back-the-freak-up presence as a black male. From some men who crossed my path, I took the fire that for me symbolizes black manhood. And from others, the gentle hand, tenderheartedness, and righteousness that is our eternal flame. From my father, even in his absence, or perhaps because of it, what I took was the memory of a father walking hand in hand with a son, the smell of cinnamon gum, and a pact that I made with myself to be a better man than he was. In letting go of my anger as I sat talking with my father's mother, as it seeped from my pores like sweat and spilled from my heart and soul, I was also filled with sympathy and sorrow for my father, whom I was beginning to see as a troubled boy who grew up to be a troubled man whose troubles eventually swallowed him up whole.

Before we left Evergreen that next morning, there was one last stop to make on my journey. I needed to go by Long Corner Cemetery to see where my father was buried. Mrs. Jackson said that one of her sons would need to take me by the cemetery, not far from her house. It wasn't the cemetery that she feared I would have trouble finding but rather my father's grave, which was not marked with a headstone. At the cemetery, my father's younger brother, Billy, led me to the gravesite and after a while, narrowed my father's resting place to one of several nameless white slates covered by weeds and grass.

"I think it's this one," he said, looking puzzled. "But I can't say for sure."

I stood above the grave, teary-eyed. Then I squatted. Billy and my wife and son walked away so that I could make my peace.

I had not been able to cry at his funeral. But sixteen years later, the tears began to pour. They flowed freely as I began to have that long-overdue conversation that I had always dreamed of having with my father. Much of what I said at the gravesite that day remains a blur, though I do recall telling him who I was, telling him about the man I had become.

It was only those words that I found most liberating that I clearly remember saying: "I love you, Dad," I said, wiping away tears, "And I forgive you."

With that said, I climbed into my car and drove out of Long Corner Cemetery, away from Evergreen, away from death and back toward life.

Making Me Whole—
Memories of Grandpa

Anne Valente

The bullet splintered the white plaster wall above the blanketed couch in my grandparents' basement, the mark's jagged edges surrounding a dark, hollow cavity that was never repaired. It remained dormant and neglected, as though mending it would concede what had happened. Its presence alone meant my absence thereafter, from the basement where my older sister Michelle and I had once watched Saturday morning cartoons and built furniture forts, hiding inside our enclosed havens with flashlights and blankets.

It was a dime-sized, concrete reminder that those moments were over, tangible evidence that in December of 1997, exactly two weeks before Christmas, my grandfather retreated downstairs in the middle of the night and, enclosed deep within the silence of walls that he had himself built, willfully ended a struggle he could no longer endure.

Lung cancer was the struggle, an acutely aggressive form of it caused by the asbestos my grandpa never knew he was inhaling as he built the churches of Alton, Illinois–grand brick structures that today bear witness to the careful hands that once crafted them. The damage showed only years later, when tiny tumors began to attack the pleural lining of his lungs and, just several short months after that, metastasized in baseball size to his back.

Once the pain grew too intense to handle, the tumors forced my grandpa from his favorite end of their paisley-yellow couch—molded gently over time to the shape of his body, and the imprint of my grandmother's on the other end—to the harder, sturdy-backed wooden chairs in their living room. He gave up his spot like the gentleman he was, an insistence that emanated in soft tones from his forever calm voice. But I never felt comfortable taking his place.

And then, one night that December, Grandpa took a loaded gun from his days as a soldier in World War II, proceeded downstairs, and ended that pain–and the humiliation I know he felt, of dependence and of perceived burden to us–with a single bullet.

The path that bullet made, charted in one isolated moment, forced me for years from everything that came before its violent divide. It hardened me against my own memories, driving them forcefully underground.

But now, as I sit here with my pen in hand—and with a small teapot filled with jasmine tea—I know this hollowed hole is not what I remember. Instead, I remember everything else—everything within the fabric of my memory that has woven the complicated patchwork of the man my grandfather was.

I remember him as the cause behind the eternally reassuring smell of cinnamon raisin toast, its scent drifting into my mother's old bedroom to wake me each time we stayed at my grandparents' house. My grandpa fancied himself a cinnamon toast aficionado, browning and buttering each slice with his patient hands, and each morning he seated himself at the kitchen table across from my sister and me, waiting good-naturedly alongside a toaster plugged into the wall.

Grandpa engaged us in morning chitchat, asking about our forays into the wilderness behind their brick home and about our science projects at school. He also tolerated the growing pile of crusts on my plate that I refused to eat. His whiskered, sandpapery face lit up each time one of us requested another slice of "roach bread," the nickname he lent our breakfast for the way the dark raisins resembled tiny bugs. He chuckled, his brown eyes crinkling at the corners, whenever we bristled at the name.

He was also a master of grilled corn, its savory flavors wrapped in tin foil and roasted over the barbecue pit in the backyard while he stood watch with a pair of metal tongs. He always cut the corn from the cobs for my sister and me—standing them on end and carving, their kernels falling in neat blocks to the plate—to spare any loose baby teeth from catching on the cob's tough core. If it was a particularly special evening, orange soda floats followed as an after-dinner treat. We always had them in the kitchen to avoid spilling on the carpet, then retired to the living room for episodes of *The Golden Girls,* a comforting prelude to being tucked in for the night. The floats' bubbly foam was my favorite part, surrounding the lump of vanilla ice cream as it bobbed in a sea of orange fizz.

If orange soda and ice cream didn't happen to be in the fridge, we walked to the Cream Machine instead. My grandpa loved going on "nature walks" with us, on which he pointed out bird and plant species as they happened across our path, and the ice cream stand at the end of their street served as a convenient destination for after-dinner strolls on summer evenings. My sister and I often couldn't resist running ahead, the crunch of gravel crackling beneath our feet as we scrambled up the unpaved lane amid humming cicadas and fading twilight.

Nature walks sometimes turned into daylong trips up the Great River Road, Alton's scenic thoroughfare along the banks of the Mississippi River. As we navigated the road's weaving contours, we scanned barren trees for nesting bald eagles in the snowy cold of January, and we stopped at fried catfish stands in the warmth of June.

Grandpa also took us fishing in Alton, in the lakes of the Sportsmen's Club, and my favorite part was stopping at the bait shop along the way. Grandpa sometimes cracked open the Styrofoam container so we could peek at the heap of tangled earthworms inside, and I loved staring into the shop's cage of buzzing crickets. Michelle and I divided front-seat privileges in Grandpa's beige Buick, she on the way there, and me on the way back.

I remember Grandpa as a man in his own right as well, harboring qualities outside the realm of who he might have been as a grandfather but which shade for me the gradations of his identity. He was a great dancer, and he also played on the soldiers' baseball team while he was stationed in Naples during World War II. He often ate salted peanuts on the back porch as he listened to Cardinals games on a crackling, hand-held radio, and he tucked my mother into bed every night when she was a little girl.

Grandpa relished his retirement years, taking up the cultivation of bonsai trees and sketching as hobbies, and traveling with my grand-mother to Egypt and France on funds they had long saved for that pur-pose. He was also a romantic, which hit me with subtle warmth when I learned that my grandmother once mailed him a handwritten poem when he was stationed in Italy during the war. He kept that poem in his wallet for over fifty years, its edges yellowed and worn.

I have kept many things as well, including a small box of mementos hidden in the uppermost shelves of my bedroom closet. I, too, now hold that poem my grandmother wrote so many years ago, retyped by my grandfather and delivered to each of us as a parting love poem shortly before he died.

I retain the letters he sent me years ago while I was at summer camp, a collection of notes printed in his boxy, all-caps handwriting. There is another to which I also cling, written in the same, neat script—the final letter he wrote in the weeks before his passing.

"If I should ever leave you and go along the silent way, grieve not," he wrote. "When you hear a song or see a bird I loved, please do not let the thought of me be sad, for I am loving you as I always have."

This is the man he was. And my burden, the guilt of allowing a bul-let hole to cloud my memory of him for so many years.

When I see a bright red cardinal perched in a tree that reminds me of our nature walks, I think of the man who held my hand as I crossed the street to the Cream Machine, of the master of grilled corn, of the ro-mantic who took care not to scratch my grandmother with his sandpa-pery whiskers when he kissed her.

I hope my grandpa knows that this is what I remember. I also hope he knows that there is no forgiveness to bestow. I hope he knows that although I cannot promise that I don't still grieve, it is not for the way he left us.

Anne Valente—A native Missourian, she grew up in St. Louis, just across the Mississippi River from her grandparents in Alton, Illinois. She received a B.A. in English literature and film studies from Washington University, and an M.S. in journalism from the University of Illinois at Urbana-Champaign. She currently teaches composition and creative writing in Ohio and serves as the assistant editor of the literary magazine *Storyglossia*. Her varied literary and journalistic works have appeared in a number of publications, including *Sauce Magazine, Playback St. Louis, Keyhole Magazine, Monkeybicycle, Fiction Weekly, Pank Magazine,* and the *Washington Post.*

The Father in Me

Lee Bey

The Dream

I walk into the kitchen. My father is there, dressed for work; the afternoon sun, shining golden through a pattern of the kitchen windows.

"Daddy," I say.

"How you doing, Chip?" he said, calling me by the nickname my mother gave me.

"I miss you," I tell him. "We all miss you."

My father was Lee J. Bey. He loved us all. My mother, Lula; my older sisters, Claudette and Deneterius. Our relatives. When I was a small child in the late 1960s and early 1970s, he'd pack our kinfolk in his car and bring them over to our house. The food, the laughter, the music. And my father, handsome and funny, holding court over it all.

My father and I were the only males in a house full of women. We were virtually inseparable. Unless I was at school, or running the sidewalks with my friends, I was with him, picking up the tricks and lessons of manhood.

One lesson I learned: *Don't back down from a fight.* Another: *Don't take no mess.* When I was about three or four, one of my aunts brought an unruly and disrespectful boyfriend to a party we hosted. My father wound up throwing the man out the door and down the front steps of our house at 7327 South Kimbark. On his way to the pavement, the boyfriend cleared eight wide wooden steps (plus the concrete first step), hit the ground, and broke his ankle.

When I was twelve, I punched out an older bully who tried to steal a ride from my bike. My father smiled when he heard about it. "Sometimes you have to show people," he said.

He wore his manhood without much bluff or bluster. "You can't tell somebody you are a man," he used to tell me. "You are. Or you aren't."

I wanted to be just like him. I wanted to be a man.

"How's your mother?" my father asks.
"She's sad," I say. "She took it hard."
"I know."

The Kiss

My father's friends drank, smoked, and cursed. They fixed cars and figured stuff out. I was an honorary member of this closed society, even when I was as young as four or five. They called me Chip or "Lil' Bey," gave me 7-Up or Canada Dry. I couldn't have been happier. From my father and his friends, I learned about fraternity, politics, and sometimes, women.

When I was about eight, my father and his oldest brother, George, and I went to see their friend Jimmy. We got there and while the men were greeting each other, Jimmy's pretty wife pulled me aside, kissed me smack on the lips and told me I had pretty eyelashes. *Oh, I was a man, now,* I mused to myself.

I silently reveled in the kiss on the drive back while my father and uncle recapped the visit. Then, my Uncle George said with disgust: "Why his wife always want to put her lips on somebody? I didn't let her kiss me."

"Me either," my father said. "To tell you the truth, don't nobody know *where* her mouth been."

Oh no! My eight-year-old imagination conjured images of Jimmy's wife eating out of garbage cans, kissing brick walls in dark alleys, and licking jelly off the floor when nobody was looking. I couldn't swallow for the rest of the trip home.

"You okay back there, boy?" one of them would say.

"Ummm hmmm," I grunted, not wanting to swallow, unable to spit and afraid to tell them that Jimmy's wife had got me.

Passings

When I got older, my father and I didn't get along. In seventh and eighth grade, I barely studied and was disruptive in class, got poor marks. During a parents' conference, he noticed that my seat was separated from the rest of the class.

"My son is sitting in the nigger seat," he told me. "Nigger" was a curse word in our house, reserved for the black person who refused to behave, who refused to achieve. The remark was meant to sting. It did.

I got admitted to a top public high school in 1979 but was still a horrible student, which caused more problems between me and my father. Meanwhile, I had begun to resent his drinking. By then older, he became much different when he drank: Sullen. Crabby. Joyless. I sometimes hated coming home.

By 1981, my father had retired and my parents opened Bey's Grocery at Eighty-seventh Street and South Chicago Avenue. Our small store struggled. So my father went to work as a security guard to make ends meet. But the iciness between us eventually thawed. We started hanging out again, went on long drives and talked. And I looked forward to the time we spent together.

Then one day early that August, my father came home from work. I knew something was wrong; just the way the air moved. I ran to the backyard to see what was wrong. He sat motionless in his car, the driver's side door open, his feet on the ground.

"Go get your mother," he said. I did.

My mother took him to the hospital. The doctors found problems with his intestines and removed yards of them. I got to see him a few days after the operation. In a sterile hospital room, he lay connected to an elaborate maze of wires and hoses. But he could talk.

"Hey, Chip" he said, weak but cheerful.

"Hey, Daddy," I said, fighting to stay strong, whispering silently inside: *Gotta be a man now. No crying. None of that.* "How are you?" I asked.

"I'm okay," he said.

My father didn't want me to see him that way, I could tell.

Then the nurses appeared. They had to do something, so I had to leave. I stepped out of his hospital room, into the corridor with still so many unspoken words between a father and his son, but still with hopes of making a lifetime of moments and memories. But I knew time was not on our side. So did he.

I never got to say another word to my father. Not even a proper good-bye.

Does he know I love him? I wondered the day he died. *What happens next? What am I supposed to do now?*

My father died August 19, 1981. He was fifty-two. I was fifteen. The funeral was at the Major-Miller Funeral Home, a converted 1920s bank on West Seventy-ninth Street.

I looked at my father in the gray metal casket. Even now, more than twenty-five years later, I can still see the dab of moisture that resembled a tear on the bottom eyelashes of his closed right eye. A spasm of sadness rushed over me as I stood above him that day: a man's man, lying tearfully in his coffin.

The service was hot and endless. My sisters, my cousins, my father's friends—all of the people who had laughed so richly when we'd gathered together when he was alive—were all glum and ashen.

At one point, the attendant tried to close the casket but the lid slipped from his hand and slammed shut. I flinched. The finality of it all. I wanted to cry.

When they closed the casket again at the end of the service, my mother—a rock—broke down. "Lee?" she called out to my father. "*Leeee!*" she cried as she spread her arms and soul atop the closed coffin. It is what we were all feeling that day. Only she was truthful enough to fully express it.

The Dream

A month after the funeral, I dreamed about my father. To this day, it is the most vivid and detailed dream I've ever had:

I open a door in the house where we live, only to find myself in the kitchen of that house on Kimbark Avenue. My father is there, dressed for work. The afternoon sun shines golden through the kitchen windows. My mother has gotten up from the table, but her coffee cup is still here. A filterless Pall Mall is sitting in the ashtray near the center of the table, next to my father's cup of black coffee. I stand behind him. The two of us have the kitchen to ourselves.

"Daddy," I say, more surprised than anything.

"How you doing, Chip?" he asks.

"I miss you," I tell him. "We all miss you."

"How's your mother?" he asks, though he never quite turns around in his chair.

"She's sad," I say. "She took it hard."

"I know," he says. "And how are your sisters?"

"Claudette and Charles are back in Florida," I tell him. "Deneterius is back in college."

He nods, almost like he knows, but wants—needs—to hear it for confirmation.

"But you?" I ask.

"I'm alright," he answers. "I want you to know I'm all right."

I begin to cry.

"What am I going to do?" I ask. "I ... I ... I don't know what to do."

Then suddenly, my father turns toward me. Not fully. But I can see more of his profile.

"You are going to be alright," he says, reassuring. "You are going to make it."

"There is a lot I want to ask … that I want to say," I tell him.

"I know," he says. "But you don't have enough time now."

Just then, I notice the door I had walked through—which is behind me—that the door is slowly beginning to close.

"You better get on back through there," my father urges me. "The time is running out."

I hear him. But I want to touch him. Hug him. Feel his hand once again on my shoulder.

"Chip, you going to be fine," he says. "You have to get back through the door."

Reluctantly, I step back through the door, crying.

From the dream that morning, I awakened only to discover that my tears were real.

Epilogue

The old man was correct, as usual. I turned out okay. I've been a newspaper reporter, a top mayoral adviser, a senior staffer at a major architecture firm, and I am now executive director of a major downtown civic group. My marriage failed after sixteen years, but out of it, I have three beautiful daughters and a great stepson. As my girls grow older, I see shades of my father in them. The way they express surprise—the smart-aleck comments they whip out. And I can't help but laugh.

I walk and mingle with the city's most influential people. My father taught me how to do that. But I can also make my children laugh until their sides ache because he taught me that, too.

I *wish* he could have lived to see it all. But maybe, just maybe he somehow already knew the outcome. At least a son can hope.

LEE BEY—Writer, prize-winning architectural critic and photographer, he was formerly a reporter-columnist for the *Chicago Sun-Times*. By 1997, Bey had become one of Chicago's foremost architectural critics, writing about issues of architecture and urban planning in his weekly column for the *Sun-Times*. A Chicago native son, Bey was formerly top aide to Mayor Richard M. Daley and is currently executive director of the Chicago Central Area Committee, a civic organization of prominent downtown businesspeople concerned with the architecture, urban planning, transportation, and economic viability of the Loop. He lectures widely on issues of urban development and architectural preservation.

If I Had Had a Father

John W. Fountain

If I had had a father who would have given me more than a name
If I had had a father whose love I could fully claim
If I had had a father
Just to hold my hand
To show me as a little boy how I should be a man …
If I could have come to know him
Face to face
As father and son,
I wonder how much more I'd be
How much faster I might have run.
How much surer I would stand as a man
How much more confident I would be
Rather than too often wounded by failure
Eyes too clouded by hurt to see:
Possibility
My love-ability
My vulnerability—as strength
Rather than as weakness
My proneness for gentleness
My meekness

How fewer times I might have been overwhelmed
By feelings of insufficiency
That sometimes made me speak less
That sometimes made me feel less
Be less like me.
If I were more than the image of him
Long faded from the mirror of my mind
If I had had a father who had only whispered back in kind:
"I love you."
"I believe in you."
"I'm here for you."
"You don't stand alone."
I imagine I might never have known
The loneliness I've known
Of being on one's own
Or the shadows that sometimes haunt boys—and girls
Long after they are grown
That hole called fatherlessness
That still makes men—and women—groan.
I might have never known
If I had had a father.

Afterword

John W. Fountain

He was his only son. And of all the brutality, sordid details, and assorted facts that fell upon my ears that day like hot coals, it was that one truth that has forever singed my soul. It happened while I was a reporter at the *Chicago Tribune* in the early 1990s, on a day when I was sitting in on cases being heard at the Cook County Criminal Courthouse on Twenty-sixth Street and California Avenue in search of a daily story and stumbled upon a most horrifying case. I sat captivated and at the same time disturbed by the details of a father accused of slaying his only son.

Apparently angry with the child's mother, who, as I remember, wasn't home at the time of the incident, the father, according to prosecutors, had filled a bucket with scalding-hot water and placed his toddler son inside—held him tightly while his son screamed and his skin melted, then laid him on a bed where it was believed the child suffered alone in searing agony until he died. I wasn't there to hear his screams. But they seemed to rise from the riveting, detailed portrait of murder at the hands of a merciless killer, painted by prosecutors.

That anyone could do something so inhumane and sadistic to any living creature, let alone a child, was unconscionable. That a father might do this to a son, even his only son, made the day that I came into the knowledge of this case among my most miserable as a journalist. While covering crime and murder and mayhem, I routinely encountered numerous nightmarish true tales. But the details of this one made me sick to my stomach. And as I stared at the father, who was sitting behind the defendant's table, I had thoughts I cannot mention, and I felt toward him only rage.

Although the scalding slaying of which I speak is undoubtedly an extreme case, various degrees of paternal neglect, abuse, and failure span the continuum of fatherhood. At the opposite end are good and loving fathers, who, mistakes notwithstanding, seek to nurture, nourish, and steer their children to adulthood. They are men who understand that fathering entails making financial provision. But they also understand that though we fathers provide the financial wherewithal for our children, that this is not the sufficiency of fatherhood and never a substitute for our love, our time, and our devotion. I have long understood this as a father and have endeavored to faithfully and fully honor this calling known as fatherhood.

I believe that we have no calling greater than fathering our own children, and none more encompassing or more challenging. I have known disappointment as a son abandoned by a father. And I have also known disappointment as a father who has often felt unappreciated and undervalued by my older children. And yet, this much I have come to understand: That we are not responsible for our father's failings to embrace us, nor for any of our children's failure to embrace or honor us as fathers. That being a good father is not contingent on any reward, even one as simple as honor and respect. And that to be a good father is honor enough in itself and a good and faithful calling. That calling is not contingent upon whether our relationships with the mother of our children endure, neither on what new love, opportunity, challenge, or hardship arises in our lives as the world turns. And even if it is the case that we have failed or fallen down on the job, we must now, right now, decide to get up and begin anew. The stakes are too high.

I have always wanted to be a good father. I don't know if this was as much innate as it was born by the desertion of my natural father, by the countless days of futilely waiting as a boy on the front porch for him to return, or his absence from the seats at my basketball games, from the stands at track fields, or from the audience at graduations. Inasmuch as it stemmed from my own desire to be a good father—a good man— my drive was steeped in my own pain as a child who craved a long-gone father's embrace, and also a prepubescent vow that my own children would never know such pain, would never have to search for me, never have to sift the darkest corners of their mind for memories of their father's face. I vowed not to become an invisible man.

And though it is now thirty-two years later, I remember like yesterday the moment I first set eyes on my firstborn and namesake, lying swaddled in a blanket, minutes after he was born that summer evening. I remember vividly each of my five children's births. More important, I have been there, endeavoring to produce, provide, and protect, though sometimes admittedly falling short along this roadway called life, with its many unexpected twists and turns. Through their falls, scrapes, and spills, through a lifetime of parent-teacher conferences, field trips, hospital visits, school plays, recitals, and myriad other events and functions; through divorce and heartache, through good times and bad times.

It has not been easy. Parenting never is. And whether I have been a good father ultimately is not for me to say. For as fathers, we are not the best or most crucial assessors of how well we have kept the unspoken charge we owe to our children. This much, however, I think every father, at the end of the day, should be able to say: That I have done all I know as a father. That I have endeavored to do better when I have come into that knowledge. That my mistakes are never an excuse. And that I have exhaustedly poured my heart, mind, and soul into loving and caring for my children.

As fathers, we must also learn to say, "I'm sorry." To seek forgiveness, and yet to try from the start to avoid those regrettable, hard-to-forgive, and egregious inflictions that can so indelibly stain our children. And we must forgive ourselves, though the prospect of forgiveness and the miracle of grace must never abdicate personal responsibility.

A call to responsible fatherhood without condemnation is what is needed to redeem those men who have vacated their vocation as their children's paternal guide, to help restore those fathers who have failed or fallen down on the job. A celebration of fatherhood and unbridled praise of those men who, though less than perfect, embrace their role as fathers, is what is needed—for our posterity and the restoration of the institution to its rightful place as being among the most sacred of life's callings.

I was reminded of this as I read each of the essays in this compilation, moved in different ways by the writers' sharing memories of their fathers. Empowered by the words of Don Hayner, whose father's wisdom, spoken amid the agony of bereavement, many years later still rings in a son's heart. Reminded of the hope of reconciliation for as long as there is breath and life—a truth made clear by Sylvester Monroe's story of reconnecting with a father thought long lost in a war, finally united with a son, a reunion sweetened by baseball on a summer day and the kindling of new memories.

I was reminded of the soaring possibilities of the human spirit to supersede circumstance inherent in the moving stories of Stephanie Gadlin and Lolly Bowean—and both of which spoke to me of the resilience of little girls and their ability, despite the weaknesses or shortcomings of the men who should have fathered them, to grow into strong women. I was reminded of the cementing bond of love and healing through Joe Kirby's moving tribute to a not-so-tough-as-nails father, through Anne Valente's remembrance of a loving grandfather beyond the bullet hole that reminded her of the way he left them, by Lee Bey's recollections of the lessons, life, and breath of a father lost too soon but forever embedded in the heart, soul, and psyche of a son.

In this collection, I was reminded that there are so many good fathers, and sadly, that there are also many who are not so good. And yet I was also reminded that there is hope. For fathers and for the children.

I cannot say what the hope is for that father who placed his son in that bucket whose story I encountered while a reporter years ago at the *Tribune*. I do know that mortal hope did not save his son. I also know that the tales and transcripts of the lives between us and our fathers may be riddled with the kind of hurt and disappointment that may seem too difficult to overcome.

But I believe we can, that we must, for our own sake and for the sake of our children and our children's children—whether we indeed ever reconcile with our fathers or not. We must make—find—peace. An understanding that this is more about us than it is about them is half the battle.

I made my peace with my father in painstaking increments over the years, through the slow untangling of hurts, and finally with a long overdue, tearful conversation while standing above his unmarked grave. My hope is that those who need it will find the kind of peace resonant in the words of many of the writers here. My hope is that those who lack fathers or fathering will find strength, solace, and reassurance in the stories of some writers here whose paternal hurt became their stepping stone. My hope is that others will be moved to become better fathers—spurred by the memories and examples of good fathers, crystallized by some writers here. That because of this book some fathers will be encouraged to stay the course, despite the urge to veer and those seemingly endless, sometimes thankless and mundane duties of fatherhood. That because of this book fathers will be reminded that the most critical resources required for being a good father are your heart and your time.

My hope is also that everyone with a good father will tell them—remind them—how much they are loved and appreciated. And should you by chance find words too awkward to speak, may I humbly suggest that you begin in your own quiet place with a pen and a blank sheet of paper by writing these two simple words: "Dear Dad."

Acknowledgments

I am most grateful to every contributor to this work, and I shall forever call each of them "friend." Thank you for sharing your stories, for opening the curtains on the windows of your world, and for entrusting me with your gift.

My thanks to Janis Kearney, Joshua Pondexter, and Jim Davis for your selfless support and advice at a time when I was contemplating taking the plunge into publishing. Thanks to my friends at Starbucks in Matteson, Illinois (especially, Terri, Donna, Randy, Melvin, and all the men of the "Round Table"), without whose daily dosages of laughter and contagious zest for life I might become a workaholic. Thank you, Will Parker, for speaking in faith about my future and about my hopes as an author and publisher.

A special thanks to all of those who didn't believe in me and whose doubt and naysaying shall continue to be my oxygen as I strive for higher heights. And thanks to all who in love and goodwill have supported me in my endeavors and vision.

Thank you to the late professor Bob Reid, whose words of wisdom over the years and whose faith in me spring eternal.

Thank you to Laura Sebold, whose inspiring cover nailed my vision for a face for *Dear Dad*. To Terry Musclow at Dickinson Press, whose publishing knowledge and kindness were our compass at critical times during this project. And a special thanks to Michele Wynn—only the world's greatest editor—who also edited my book *True Vine* and who graciously took on this work. Many thanks as well to attorney Henry R. Kaufman for your legal eyes and counsel.

To my stepfather, Eddie Clincy, who is my dad. And to every man who purposely poured into my life. To my grandmother, Florence Hagler, who stirred my faith and wished me only good. And to my grandfather, George Hagler, who taught me to stand as a man. Thank you to my sister Meredith and Aunt Clotee, my most loyal supporters. And thank you to my brother Jeff and my sister Gloria, always loving and in my corner.

To Monica, Imani, and Malik, who have been my anchors and with whom I have launched with great expectations WestSide Press, a division of FountainsWorks. Thank you, Monica, too, for your eyes on this project.

And finally, to my mother, Gwendolyn Clincy, who at times in my life has been my refuge, at other times my protector, and who is forever my first love.

My thanks to God and His Son Jesus Christ are without saying. For without Him, I could do nothing. He is perfect. The mistakes—all of them—are mine. To Him be glory.

Editor's Biography

A native son of Chicago, John W. Fountain is an award-winning journalist, professor, and author of the memoir *True Vine: A Young Black Man's Journey of Faith, Hope, and Clarity* (PublicAffairs 2003; paperback March 2005). He is currently a professor at Roosevelt University and a weekly columnist for the *Chicago Sun-Times*.

In a journalism career that has spanned twenty years, Fountain has been a reporter at some of the top newspapers in this country. From 2000 to 2003, he was a national correspondent for the *New York Times*. Based in Chicago, Fountain covered a twelve-state region. He has also been a staff writer at the *Washington Post* and the *Chicago Tribune*. He has written for the *Wall Street Journal, Chicago Sun-Times, Modesto Bee, Pioneer Press Newspapers* in suburban Chicago, and the *Champaign News-Gazette*.

Until fall 2007, he was a tenured full professor at his alma mater, the University of Illinois at Urbana-Champaign, where he had taught for the previous three years. Professor Fountain was formerly a visiting scholar at the Medill School of Journalism at Northwestern University in Evanston.

In addition to working as a national correspondent, Fountain has been a crime and courts reporter as well as a general assignment reporter and features writer. Described by peers and readers as a gifted storyteller, he has won the praise of colleagues and the community for his insightful writing and reporting. Fountain has won numerous honors for feature writing from the National Association of Black Journalists, the Associated Press, the American Association of University Women, and the Society of Professional Journalists and has received the New York Times Publisher's Award for his coverage of the Mississippi River Flood. In 2003, he was a finalist in feature writing and sports writing for the Peter Lisagor Award for excellence in journalism.

Fountain frequently speaks to inner-city youth and other groups. He shares his inspirational story of going from poverty and the urban mean streets of Chicago's West Side to the top of his profession. Fountain earned his bachelor's and master's degrees from the University of Illinois at Urbana-Champaign. In 1999, Fountain was one of twelve American journalists selected for the prestigious Michigan Journalism Fellowship for the 1999–2000 class at the University of Michigan in Ann Arbor. Fountain studied inner-city poverty and race.

Fountain grew up on some of the meanest streets in Chicago, where drugs, crime, decay, and broken homes consigned so many black children to a life of despair and self-destruction. A father at seventeen, a college dropout at nineteen, a welfare case soon after, Fountain was on the verge of giving up all hope. One thing saved him—his faith, his own true vine.

Fountain's stories and essays continue to appear in news publications across the country and overseas, including his poignant essay "No Place for Me," on his disenchantment with the "Black Church," a commentary first published in the *Washington Post* and subsequently in newspapers across the country, including the *Dallas Morning News, Atlanta Journal-Constitution, Chicago Sun-Times, Louisville Courier,* and *Biloxi Sun Herald,* among others, and which sparked discussions across the country.

From the Founder and Publisher

Publishing is for me a lifelong dream, a calling to inspire change and understanding, a way of rekindling hope and healing. My goal is to make perhaps my corner of the world just a little brighter through the powerful gift of storytelling.

In addition to the conventional book format, we here at WestSide Press will produce literature in a variety of electronic formats, including podcasts, audio books, videos, and electronic books, in an effort to bring to you our stories in whatever way you desire to consume them. For we understand that even in a new and technologically evolving and exciting age there still exists an age-old thirst for a good story. We intend to evolve with that process, seeking to remain relevant, current, and in tune with these changing times.

Many of the faces and voices that appear in the stories will be black and brown. But they are stories that run far deeper than one's skin color or ethnicity. They are stories that center on fundamental universal truths and our collective commonality as members of that one true race known as the human race.

In 1985, the *Chicago Tribune* published a series dubbed *The American Millstone*. The newspaper deemed the people of the city's West Side community known as North Lawndale—where I grew up—as the "permanent underclass." We were, in the *Trib's* view, the millstone draped around America's neck. I was a resident of the West Side at the time the *Trib's* reporters came a'calling.

I cannot subscribe to their assessment of the state of destitution they perceived and ultimately portrayed in their stories. And yet the West Side has been my scar for life, like growing up on the other side of the tracks, the thing that people point to as evidence of my lack of pedigree, a place perceived to be so bathed in poverty and despair as to render it and its inhabitants forever hopeless, as being "less than."

I once heard a preacher say half-jokingly, "Can any good thing come from the West Side?"—echoing a sentiment expressed in the Bible about a rabbi from Nazareth.

So in contemplating a name for this publishing company, it seemed only logical to call it something that would for me embody struggle but also hope, despair but also determination, resistance but also resilience, both poverty and promise; a name that would speak to the value and validity of the stories of every "West Side" on earth—from North Lawndale to a squatter's camp in Soweto, to Palestine and Pembroke, Illinois.

I needed a name that might say to anyone who has ever felt discarded, "Yes, you can." A glorious name grafted in pain, born through shame, once a burden and now my gain. And I could think of none better than WestSide Press.

For every dark corner and for places like the West Side of Chicago, where the media light too seldom shines unless it is to spotlight the bad, I publish. For anyone seeking the truth and the stories of those seldom seen or heard, I publish. For you, I publish. Welcome to WestSide Press.

JOHN W. FOUNTAIN